Stories from the Rains of Love and Death

Four Plays from Iran

Stories from the Rains of Love and Death

Four Plays from Iran

Aurash

The Death of the King

by Bahram Beyza'ie

Stories from the Rains of Love and Death

by Abas Na'lbandian

Interrogation

by Mohammad Rahmanian

Translated by Soheil Parsa, with Peter Farbridge and Brian Quirt

Playwrights Canada Press
Toronto • Canada

Stories from the Rains of Love and Death: Four Plays from Iran © copyright 2008 Soheil Parsa
Introduction © copyright 2007 Dr. Mahmood K. Moghaddam
For individual titles, please see opposite page.
The authors assert moral rights.

Playwrights Canada Press
The Canadian Drama Publisher
215 Spadina Avenue, Suite 230, Toronto, Ontario CANADA M5T 2C7
416-703-0013   fax 416-408-3402
orders@playwrightscanada.com • www.playwrightscanada.com

This book would be twice its cover price were it not for the support of Canadian taxpayers through the Government of Canada Book Publishing Industry Development Programme, the Canada Council for the Arts, the Ontario Arts Council and the Ontario Media Development Corporation.

 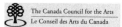

Front cover painting "Painting by Shirin Ghandchi, from her series, "Stepping Out"
www.aliandshirin.com
Production editor/cover design: JLArt

Library and Archives Canada Cataloguing in Publication

Beyza'ie, Bahram
    Stories from the rains of love and death : four plays from Iran / translated by Soheil Parsa, with Peter Farbridge and Brian Quirt.

Translated from Arabic.

Contents: Aurash / by Bahram Beysa'ie ; translated and adapted by Soheil Parsa with Brian Quirt ; edited by Peter Farbridge. -- The death of the king / by Bahram Beyza'ie ; translated by Soheil Parsa with Peter Farbridge. -- Stories from the rains of love and death / by Abas Na'lbandian ; translated by Soheil Parsa with Peter Farbridge. -- Interrogation / by Mohammad Rahmanian ; translated by Soheil Parsa.
ISBN 978-0-88754-819-2

    1. Arabic drama--Iran. I. Parsa, Soheil II. Farbridge, Peter, 1967- III. Quirt, Brian IV. Na'lbandian, Abas V. Rahmanian, Mohammad VI. Title.

PJ7916.E99S7613 2008   892.727   C2008-901048-5

First edition: February 2008.
Printed and bound by Canadian Printco at Scarborough, Canada.

Dedication

While I deeply respect the work of these three important playwrights from Iran, I would like to dedicate this work to playwright Bahram Beyza'ie. In my development as a theatre artist, Bahram Beyza'ie figures as a central character. Beyza'ie's profound knowledge of theatre, his dedication to his craft, his humanist vision, and the simplicity and rich imagery of his plays have been instrumental to my growth as an artist and as a human being. And despite the great restrictions placed on him in his country, his work continues to inspire other artists such as myself all over the world.

Soheil Parsa
Artistic Director
Modern Times Stage Company

Acknowledgements

The translators would like to thank: the actors of the first productions
of these plays, whose feedback fed the final versions of the translations; the
Canada Council for the Arts, the Ontario Arts Council, the Toronto Arts Council
and the Laidlaw Foundation for their financial support; Bahram Beyza'ie and
Mohammed Rahmanian for trusting us with their work; Guillermo Verdecchia
for his editing comments; as well as special thanks to Azita Parsa, Jahan Parsa,
Joan Farbridge and Nancy Webster for their important personal support.

Table of Contents

FOUR PLAYS FROM IRAN

An introduction by
Dr. Mahmood K. Moghaddam

• • •

The history of theatre in Iran has been, as Thomas Hardy said of life, "a long drama of pain with short episodes of happiness in it." Painstaking contributions to the genre, therefore, including the collection in this volume, are unquestionably valuable commodities.

The very title *Four Plays from Iran* may evoke in a Persian reader the notion that drama is a less prestigious literary genre, at least when compared to a variety of poetic forms, for example. This is a view not limited to Persian culture, however: even when Shakespeare was at the peak of his achievements, drama did not enjoy equal prestige, and the playwright had to prove himself first and foremost in poetry, writing plays primarily to make a living.

The title *Four Plays from Iran* might also elicit a distinction in the minds of Western readers between things Western and Eastern. A general inference has often been drawn, sometimes implicitly, that things Western are somehow primary and those from the East inevitably secondary. And yet, one of the most promising sources of new thought in the Western world since the nineteenth century has been an increasing awareness of Eastern ideas. In that context, "Four Plays from Iran" can resonate with the embodiment of human experiences from a once faraway land and contribute to an ever-growing richness of culture in this part of the world.

The drama of that land, whether in its traditional forms or modern versions, has its roots first and foremost in epic literature, which has been celebrated in Iran for millennia. Its importance in the West was not recognized until the nineteenth century, when French literary criticism placed the Persian epic *Shahnameh,* or *Book of Kings*, by the poet Ferdowsi among the top five canonical works of world literature along with Homer and Shakespeare from the Western world and Valmiki and Vyasa from the Hindu tradition.

This magnificent epic tradition is still alive and a source of inspiration in Iran. Its stories and encyclopedic visions have been reflected not only in the traditional Iranian theatrical genre known as Naqqali but also in contemporary literature. The other two influences on twentieth century Persian drama have been the forms of Ta'ziyeh—a second theatrical genre—and modern European drama, especially the theatre of the absurd. The result is a gallery of modern plays benefiting both from Western dramatic forms, especially the postmodern, and from homegrown components, those rooted in cultural paradigms as well as visions arising from contemporary conditions and experiences.

Aurash, one of the four plays in this volume, is based on an episode borrowed from the Persian epic. The central character personifies a transformation of the traditional hero who, in the epic poem, contributes to his national glory by shooting an arrow farther than any hero can, in an attempt to determine the new border for his defeated nation. In this play, however, the valiant hero has been reduced to a deformed, postmodern character whose weakness will ironically reflect the work's strong antiwar, antiviolence sentiments.

The play begins at the peak of the action, displaying the horrors of war's aftermath. The army's powerful archer, Kashvad, has refused to shoot his arrow, arguing that those left beyond the point where his arrow touches the ground will be devastated by the enemy, and those on this side of the border, enslaved by their own rulers. One cannot help but be reminded of *The Iliad* and Achilles' refusal to fight. But while Achilles' rejection is designed to restore his own personal glory, in *Aurash* Kashvad refuses not for reasons of selfish gain but because of the futility of the heroic act. The meaningless deed will not free anyone from oppression stemming from within or without. This is what Aurash, the antihero, will learn in the course of the play, and together with him, the audience: "I am Aurash, the one who at the sunrise was ignorant, and now, at sunset, knows something about the world."

In the world of this play, the cycle of enslavement never ends. Aurash learns the bitter truth that your commanders will save you from the wrath of the enemy only to serve themselves, and conquerors will defeat you for similar purposes – thus the purposelessness and meaninglessness of life for those caught in this no-win situation.

Aurash, the archetype of lost humanity, exemplifies a world in which even an act of generosity is turned on its head, one in which the very existence of a saviour hero will make all others "lazy and soft," a ruthless world in which man's inhumanity to man is the game, a world that will forever "be filled with wailing of old women, the moaning of widows and the curses of those who grow old without hope." Aurash endeavours in vain, knowing "from his father that when a small scorpion is trapped in the midst of a fire, it bites itself 'til it turns into ashes. And he, Aurash, watches himself trapped in the fire of his own thoughts."

As gloomy as the theme of the play may seem, it feeds not only on the absurd of modern times but on the unique richness of the classical Persian epic's pessimistic perspective, a truth-telling philosophy that reflects man's entrapment in the combined ruthlessness of the cosmos and a world structured in such a way as to destroy humanity. In the *Shahnameh* the central character will witness his own and his nation's demise in the final episode of *Rostam and Esfandiar. Aurash,* the play, profits from this vision but also from another trend in the Persian epic best represented in the radical innocence of the *Story of Syavash* – which in turn shapes the victim mindset and martyrdom of Ta'ziyeh drama, not to mention Western absurdism. *Aurash,* in short, is a complex play, one that will not lend itself to a single "ism," benefiting rather from the combined richness of them all. The work is truly worth watching and reading.

A pessimistic outlook and the motif of man's inhumanity to man run through the other three plays in this collection. The issue here, one found in the literature of other nations as well, is the extent to which the audience/reader will want to be immersed in radically optimistic views of jingoism on the one hand and, on the other, total pessimism beyond the point of no return. The third position is to embody experiences arising from pessimistic views but also a poetic glimmering of some degree of hope. The plays in this volume revolve around the latter two possibilities, raising the question of whether humanity, when all is said and done, will be able to save itself or be totally annihilated in the physical and psychological devastation of injustice, wars and revolutions.

The ultimate effects of these plays, finally, derive not only from the original Persian texts but also from the translators' effective adaptations and the endeavours of directors, lighting designers, stage managers, and an entire chain of events associated with the process. We are fortunate to have them all.

Dr. Mahmood K. Moghaddam
Department of English
Concordia University

Translators' Note

Each of the translations of these four plays was carried out with a view to a full production at the Modern Times Stage Company. This, in many ways, shaped the spirit of the translation work, because as artist-managers in the theatre, one of our focuses was making the scripts accessible for our actors and our audience. For us then, being faithful to these scripts was not always about following every line precisely; thus this anthology should not be considered a purely literary translation.

Aurash received the strongest treatment in this regard. Bahram Beyza'ie wrote this as a one-man show, but in his preface to his play, he states he wrote the play for one or more actors. Modern Times Stage Company's production chose to stage the play with four actors, and so the translation that is in this anthology was adapted with this cast structure in mind. Beyza'ie wrote two versions of *The Death of the King* (originally *The Death of Yazdgird*), one in 1980, and a revised version in 2003; for this anthology, we updated our translation with some of Beyza'ie's revisions.

The plays were translated in a collaborative fashion. Sometimes the translation was done face to face, with the literal translation in English being read out loud, whereupon the text would be transcribed into fluid English. Many times the text was read out loud in Farsi so as to hear the rhythmic and percussive nuances in the source text that needed to be emulated in the translated version. Readings of other texts as well, including translated works of Rumi and Khayyam, helped to understand the imagistic world of the playwrights.

Soheil Parsa
Peter Farbridge
Brian Quirt
Toronto, September 2007

Aurash

Bahram Beyza'ie
Translated and adapted by Soheil Parsa with Brian Quirt
Edited by Peter Farbridge

Anna Mackay-Smith, Peter Farbridge, Ron Kennell
photo by Hassan Taheri

Aurash was first produced as a co-production with Modern Times Stage Company and Theatre Passe Muraille at the Extra Space, Toronto, from April 4 to April 30, 1998, with the following company:

A   Ron Kennell
B   Joan Heney
C   Earl Pastko
D   Todd Hammond

Direction and Choreography: Soheil Parsa
Composer: Richard Feren
Lighting Design: Philip Cygan
Set Design: Soheil Parsa and Karen Krupa
Costume Design: Soheil Parsa and Karen Krupa
Dramaturge: Brian Quirt
Stage Manager: Kathryn Davis
                              • • •

Awards and Nominations
Dora Mavor Moore Awards: Outstanding Direction of a Play (Soheil Parsa) and Outstanding Sound Design (Richard Feren). Dora Mavor Moore Nominations: Outstanding Lighting Design (Philip Cygan), Outstanding New Play–Translation and Adaptation (Soheil Parsa and Brian Quirt).

Characters

A   (plays AURASH)
B   (plays the COMMANDER and the GHOST)
C   (plays KASHVAD, HOOMANN, CORPORAL #1, the GHOST, ENEMY
     WATCHMAN #1 and the FINAL WATCHMAN)
D   (plays the GUARD, the KING, CORPORAL #2, ENEMY WATCHMAN #2 and
     the ELBORZ mountain)

All actors play choral roles as well; they are storytellers, come to retell the tale of
Aurash.

Aurash

Scene One

Music. Images of war.

A   Men came—thousands and thousands, from across the country, from far, far away—to defend their land. But none of these men would return to their homes.

C   None. And here, hearts are filled with grief, for the sky is dark, the moon is hiding, and the clouds are weeping black tears. And except for some lightning, just some lightning, there's not a glimmer of light on the warriors.

Music. Images of war.

D   The Elborz mountain—that sublime, that highest of the highs, whose peak caresses the sky, who was witness to the first revolution of the sun—sees the furious men with their feet on the ground and their heads turned to the sky, striking with their swords, striking.

Music. Images of war.

B   The Elborz, that highest, sees the men who were born in the shade of her slope, and watches them die and die. She hears their cries, aimless cries from aimless men, and is silent.

D   She knows that the lives of the people—one, two, a thousand—are worthless, worth less than the dirt on her slope.

Dead bodies cover the stage. Music.

A   And he, Aurash, the stableman, deep in thought, stares at the horizon.

D   He has just buried his horse's bloody corpse, and now he watches as red dust rising from the battlefield is swept away by the wind. He looks at the fields with sorrow, and hears a wailing, so familiar.

C   And how, we ask, how can life grow from death? Nothing grows from an earth soaked in blood. So the land became yellow, red flowers turned black, and each man, every man, was like a flower torn up in a storm.

Scene Two

A   Now through the dust

D   Comes a figure

C   Like a shadow.

B   The Commander. One foot is his: the other, wooden; a sword is his cane.

B (*as the COMMANDER*) We have agreed that by sundown our finest archer will release an arrow from the peak of the highest mountain. We have agreed that wherever that arrow lands the border of our nation will lie. Kashvad.

C Kashvad stands up like a mountain. But silent.

B You are our greatest archer and your bow is more curved than the back of the sky. Tell me, Kashvad, one arrow, one arrow of yours, if you release it with all your strength, how far would it fly?

> *Everyone looks at KASHVAD. Silence.*

You know the art of archery well, Kashvad, and your arrow has the wings of the phoenix. An arrow, an arrow of yours, if you fire it with all your might, how far would it travel?

C (*as KHASHVAD*) One parsang.

D A cry rose from the troops: "Kashvad, go, go to the enemy and tell them you will fire the arrow! And wherever your arrow lands, Kashvad, will be our border! Wherever your arrow lands!"

B Now your orders.

C I won't obey them.

B Kashvad… the wind was blowing. I couldn't hear you.

C No one man is defeated in war: we are all defeated. If I shoot this arrow I will be cursed forever. Those who remain captive, thousand upon thousand, will say that it was Kashvad's arrow that fell short and gave them to the enemy.

B We have sacrificed a hundred men for each foot of land we lost. Your arrow will redeem their loss.

C Redemption is worthless; we have lost our country.

B We have no option. This is our only hope: that with this arrow we can free more of our…

C Free?

B From slavery, Kashvad.

C Some of us were slaves before this war.

D Through the dust five guards approach.

C They haven't defeated us. We were never free. And with this arrow this will not change.

B Kashvad. Look at the enemy troops. Look at their forest of lances. We have agreed to fire an arrow to determine our border, and wherever that arrow lands, Kashvad…

C How far can an arrow travel? They know that our arrow won't fly further than our own shadows.

B The enemy will not wait for us, Kashvad: we are at their mercy.

C Thousands and thousands from coast to coast have been captured.

B We cannot free them all.

C Who led them to defeat?

A A bird cries.

D Several men fall to their knees.

A Whisperings are heard.

D And the people wail:

A "Time's running out."

D "Sundown is too soon."

A "We have lost our pride."

D "We are the scorn of the world."

B Kashvad. Pick up your bow and take the path up the mountain. This is a binding agreement; it must be executed.

C I haven't made an agreement with anyone!

   KASHVAD breaks his bow on his knee.

B This is an order.

C In defeat no one is master of the other.

B Kashvad, have you forgotten your people?

C Who is he that says I have? You, you'd gamble the millions of peoples' lives on the flight of an arrow. *(to the people around him)* This man, the one who orders me to shoot the arrow – he's tired and wants to rest – but I refuse to bargain with the enemy. I refuse to divide our people or our land. If I can't set them free, I'll stand with them and face our fate together.

D The Commander, with all his sorrow, says to the wind:

B Then tomorrow we will all be trampled.

C I will submit to the hooves of their horses, but never to this humiliation.

D And he disappears into the mist. Aurash searches for him, runs after him, calls him by name:

A *(as AURASH)* Kashvad!

D Kashvad stops, pushes the dust aside with his hand, sees Aurash there.

A   Oh valiant hero…

C   My name is Kashvad.

A   Your name is great. I have been at your side.

C   I have never seen you before.

A   I once was a shepherd in this land and now I am stableman to the troops.

C   What do you want from me, stableman?

A   I admire you, Kashvad.

C   Get away from me.

D   Kashvad fades behind the dust. A guard appears.

> (*as the GUARD*) Aurash, they're looking for a messenger to go to the enemy. I told them you know their language well. Look there!

> *The COMMANDER is summoning AURASH.*

B   You are a good stableman, Aurash, but a poor soldier. Now there are no horses left to tend, you must be our envoy with the enemy. Go, tell them: Sunset is not enough for us.

Scene Three

Music. AURASH travels to the enemy's camp. The KING and his men are celebrating their victory. AURASH arrives and bows to the KING.

B   The victorious King turns his face from the sky and looks at Aurash, his eyes burning red with the flames of the sun.

D   (*as the KING*) Was there not a single horse left alive in your land that you could ride here?

A   My horse was grazing.

D   Where? In those burnt meadows? Are you the archer?

A   No, I am the stableman of the troops and I have brought a message from our army.

D   What was the name of the previous messenger?

A   Hoomann, the valiant Hoomann.

D   Ahh… Hoomann… the valiant Hoomann. And what happened to him?

A   He didn't survive the hooves of your horses.

D   No one will survive unless he submits. Deliver your message. You have my ear.

A   One day is not enough for us: Sundown is too soon.

D   Not enough?

A   Our archer is tired.

D   Archer? Isn't that you?

A   I am a stableman.

D   But I heard you say it was you.

A   No, I did not.

D   Who is this man who calls me a liar? What was your name?

A   Aurash.

D   And you are the archer.

A   No. I have never shot an arrow in my life.

D   Excellent. Then you will fire the arrow.

A   I don't understand.

D   Yes, you do, Aurash, and you will obey.

A   I am a little man. It's not right for a king to humiliate a little man.

D   And you—a little man—would advise a king?

>   *Silence.*

Your leaders accepted this humiliation. I brought your people to their knees. You ask me to show you mercy, and I have: you and your people may live. Now you beg for land, and I offer as much land as you deserve, as much land as you can earn. Your leaders fear me, you see; it is they who have agreed.

A   We have been devastated.

D   *(laughing)* And will be more devastated when you, the one I chose, release the arrow.

A   Not me.

D   Yes, Aurash, you. We came to an agreement but we never named the archer. Now I have chosen him, and by the gods I will remain true to my word.

A   This is foolish: they will never accept me.

B   And he, the smiling King, turns to his troops—shield to shield, their ebony banners waving in the wind—and they burst into laughter. *(silence)*

D   Aurash. You know I could have killed you all.

A   Why didn't you?

D   Your people must survive to tell their children what we have bequeathed you. Wine.

A   I'm not thirsty.

D   Aurash tell me one more time – what was the name of the previous messenger, that hero of yours who died under the hooves of our horses?

A   Hoomann.

C   Hoomann. Bring Hoomann before us.

B   Aurash shivers and sees a man, like a shadow, approach from behind the red curtain of the court.

D   Hoomann, what do you know of Aurash?

C   *(as HOOMAN)* I've never heard of that name.

D   The owner of that name is here. Now look carefully and tell me: what kind of archer is he?

C   I have never seen this man among the warriors.

D   Swear it.

C   Upon my life.

D   We must write a letter, a message, Hoomann, a message in your language. *(to AURASH)* You see, he was one of you, and now he is one of our own.

B   Aurash feels his knees shaking and his eyes growing heavy. He is writhing inside. He opens his eyes, sees Hoomann standing there in front of him, and says:

A   You, our bravest warrior, we thought you were dead. Why have you betrayed us?

C   There, I was the mule of my tribe, a slave.

A   And here?

C   I have escaped from one injustice to the other, from one enemy to another. And since I am a slave, I submit to the one who feeds me better.

A   But you fought against the enemy…

C   I wanted to know if there was still love for my land in my heart, and I discovered there was none.

B   Suddenly, an insane laughter.

D   Now we must write the letter. Look up to the sky, Hoomann, the carrier pigeon is eager to fly.

A   I will go now.

D   Go, Aurash, go home, but when you arrive, you will find no friends, only strangers.

B   And now Aurash leaves and thinks about these words he has heard, but does not understand.

Scene 4

C   The sun is halfway across the sky. He, Aurash, looks up and sees a pigeon, like a white wind, streak across the blue sky. He walks through the scorched fields, and says to himself:

D   I was a simple man, tending my herd.

B   Whenever I wanted, I sang for them; whenever they slept, I rested with them.

C   How did I get here? Why has this disturbed my peace?

A   Why has this storm scattered my flock?

C   He reaches a stream but doesn't drink from it. The shade of a burnt tree invites him to rest, but he refuses. Lost in thought, he walks the dusty roads. Suddenly a wild roar like thunder breaks his solitude.

B   *(as the COMMANDER, holding the letter)* Is this true?

A   Is what true?

C   Aurash doesn't understand.

B   That is their carrier pigeon sitting on the watchtower. And this is a message with the enemy's seal.

D   And Aurash, speechless, still doesn't understand.

B   I did a foolish thing. I was told that you were an honest man, and I didn't doubt it. I noticed that you speak the language of the enemy, and I didn't get suspicious. I loved and trusted you. Why have you betrayed us?

A   I haven't.

B   Do not deny it. Here is a message from the enemy, Aurash. They will accept only one archer – you; only you. You, who are the least of men, whose arrow won't fly further than his own wretched breath.

A   Aurash has no reply. He looks around desperately, and sees five guards approaching.

B   You have pledged yourself to the enemy. This message is written in our language – written by you.

A   I don't know how to write.

B   I do not believe these words. This was written by you, and you know well what it says.

A   I don't know anything, anything.

B   I heard that you admired Kashvad for refusing to fire the arrow. Why?

A   You think I'm a traitor?

B   I have no doubt.

A   Then kill me.

B   So I will! *(He raises his sword.)*

D   Stop. If anything happens to this dog that lunatic King will have our heads.

B   This too you know, Aurash. It is written in the message. Well-planned, yes, all well-planned.

D   A guard enters and throws a bow on the ground.

C   *(as the GUARD)* This is a gift from the King to Aurash.

B   Speak, Aurash. Still you don't know anything?

D   *(as CORPORAL #2)* This belonged to Hoomann.

>   *All fall on their knees.*

B   Let us remember Hoomann, who died a man of honour. When left alone to face the enemy's countless troops, he did not submit – he shed their bodies like autumn leaves 'til his mountainous body disappeared under the hooves of their horses. This, Aurash, is the man I wish you were.

A   Then the Commander leaves, the others behind him, and Aurash is all alone, his bones aching from those words.

Scene Five

C   The beat of drums.

D   A blast of trumpets.

C   Here, under the enemy's watchtower, the corporals consult with the Commander.

>   *(as CORPORAL #1)* The watchmen of the five towers are looking out, waiting for our archer.

B   *(as the COMMANDER)* Never.

D   *(as CORPORAL #2)* That madman chose this dog. We have no choice.

C   We cannot fight this war anymore.

B   And if this animal's arrow flies no further than his own grave?

D   Whether more or less, it's not worth another bloodbath. We are tired of this war.

B   Why didn't I kill him?

C   It's not too late: he must return from the mountain sometime…

B   Ah… *(He laughs.)*

A   And they see through the dust a group of men, soldiers, with stones in their hands, following Aurash.

D   Aurash is beaten.

   AURASH is beaten by his people.

Scene Six

C   The corporal's shadow passes between the sun and Aurash.

D   *(as CORPORAL #2)* Aurash, get up, and take the bow.

C   Aurash, on his knees, hears nothing but the wind.

D   Stand up, Aurash.

B   Aurash raises his head and with his dead eyes says:

A   Were you here when they beat me like a dog?

D   Yes.

A   I haven't told them: Hoomann is still alive.

D   There is no need. We already know this.

A   You already know?

D   Yes, Hoomann is alive. In our hearts he is alive.

A   What do you want from me?

D   You know what we want.

A   I will never shoot that arrow.

D   Yes, you will, Aurash. You can refuse it again and again, but finally, you will do it.

A   Who says?

D   Won't you?

A   No.

D   And if you do not, our master will send you back to your friends upside down hanging from a mule, your hands tied, your body slashed with whips, and he will say: "It was Aurash who refused the order." Do you believe your friends will forgive you for this?

A   I have no friends. I am not on their side.

D   Is that so.

A   You won't believe me either? I can't look in the eyes of my own people anymore. Why didn't he kill me?

C   No response from the corporal.

A   What should I do? What can I do to convince you, to convince just one person?

D   I have no answer for you.

B   And now in Aurash's head something moves like lightning, like an arrow, as fast as the wind.

D   I must return to the Commander. What should I tell him?

C   Aurash stands on his feet and roars to the Elborz:

A   I will shoot the arrow!

Scene Seven

D   Drums again.

B   Trumpets again.

A   A falcon soars through the sky like a javelin.

B   And the people cry out, the people of this land with their loudest cry, say:

D   "Yes, Aurash, go, go to the enemy and tell them you will fire the arrow,

B   And wherever your arrow lands will be our land,

C   Wherever your arrow lands!"

D   And Aurash goes toward the enemy and cries:

A   "I will fire the arrow. And wherever my arrow lands will be our land."

B   And they, the enemy, they say:

C   "Yes, Aurash, draw the bow, and wherever your arrow lands will be your land."

D   But they sneered at Aurash and said to each other:

C   "How far can his arrow go?"

B   "How far can his arrow fly?"

Scene Eight

A   And he, Aurash, a man condemned by the world, says with a heart struck with grief: "How far can my arrow fly?"

> *Music. A dumb show. AURASH's people prepare him for his journey up the mountain.*

Scene Nine

D   A winding path on the mountainside. Aurash is on his way, the bow in his hands. Sunlight streaks the path before him: armed shadows lurk behind. He climbs.

Scene Ten

B   The King in his camp looks into the distance at the flames of the fire that reach to the sky with each beat of the drum. Behind him his troops: a sea of men, their flags restless in the wind. The King looks at the sun, brings his cup to his lips – the wine is bitter. Suddenly a thought, a bitter thought, trembles in his body.

D   *(as the KING)* Where is Hoomann?

C   *(as HOOMANN)* Here.

D   Hoomann. Your people have agreed that Aurash will release the arrow.

C   Fortune is on your side.

D   But they have agreed, Hoomann… don't you find that strange?

C   Why?

D   You swore he didn't know the art of archery.

C   I did.

D   Then why are they letting him climb the Elborz with his bow?

B   Hoomann is speechless.

D   Have you lied to us?

C   Never.

B   The King spills his wine on the ground. Guards approach Hoomann, waiting for the order.

D   Are you with us?

C   Am I not?

D   For a moment I thought they sent you to deceive us.

C   You will see: his arrow won't fly further than his own shadow.

D   If it does your body will be ground into red dust under the hooves of our horses.

C   It will not be so.

Scene Eleven

B   Who is this ragged little man, alone on this narrow dusty path? He burns from head to toe, his face is covered with sweat. He climbs, bow curved, string taut. Higher. Now he hears a voice. From behind a cliff a man appears.

C   Kashvad blocks his path.

  (as KASHVAD) Stop, Aurash.

A   So you have heard it, too?

C   Yes.

A   And you hate me.

C   I have come to turn you back. Thousands have died, Aurash, a hundred thousand have been captured, and you climb this mountain to save yourself.

  AURASH starts to leave.

  Listen, Aurash. Release this arrow and you save our leaders, whose deal with the enemy they claim will free our people. But with this arrow you condemn to slavery thousands upon thousands who live beyond its arc. Release this arrow, Aurash, and you divide our lands and sentence half our heart and more to our new masters.

A   Move aside.

C   Think of the people you cannot free.

A   I am one of them.

C   We have nothing but our honour, Aurash. Do not make our people slaves to your arrow.

A   I can't return, Kashvad. I am an honest man but no one believes me anymore. You, all of you, call me a liar and a traitor, so what else can I be now?

C   Aurash – I didn't believe them, but when I look at you now, I see the enemy.

A   You've just made the deepest wound; leave me alone now to suffer it.

C   Take one step more and I'll kill you.

  AURASH places his arrow in his bow, aims it at KASHVAD.

A   Listen to me, hero. I've lived a simple life, but now I've climbed beyond the fear of killing you. I have no choice. I must pass.

C   You won't kill me, Aurash.

A   Yes I will.

C   You're not an archer, Aurash – why did you agree to do this?

A   Because I want to die.

D   Kashvad moves aside, and Aurash climbs.

Scene Twelve

C   Now Aurash stands in front of Aurash.

Three AURASHes appear.

A   Stay away from me, Aurash. You stain me with myself.

B   *(as AURASH #2)* Where can I go, Aurash? I'm the only one you have. Where can you escape?

C   *(as AURASH #3)* At dawn I saw dark fortune crossing the sky, searching for somewhere to land. He was looking for you.

A   I don't deserve this.

ALL   You deserve the worst, Aurash.

D   *(as AURASH #4)* You have been condemned for your honesty and you deserve it.

B   Why didn't you flee the battlefield to the mountains?

C   Why didn't you give up your soul to a dagger?

D   Why didn't you surrender?

B   Why didn't you submit to slavery?

C   You deserve it, Aurash.

ALL   You deserve it.

A   I am simple, Aurash. Don't torture me.

C   The world mocks you, Aurash. Even your arrow will turn against you.

D   Wherever you go your people will condemn you.

B   The world will be filled with the wailing of old women, the moaning of widows, and the curses of those who grow old without hope.

ALL   And all for your deed.

A Stop, Aurash! Say no more. Don't hurt me anymore. But tell me this: this force that grows in my head, runs through my arms, races through my chest and pumps in my veins – what is this feeling in me?

ALL Think, Aurash: isn't it hopelessness?

A Yes. You're right. And I'm thankful for it. Even if my arrow falls short, even if I am shamed in front of my people, even if the whole world laughs at me, I couldn't be more disgraced than I am now.

Scene Thirteen

C The Elborz, the highest, shrouded in mist, brushed the clouds aside and saw Aurash on her slope.

D (*as the ELBORZ*) Who is this man who travels towards me with his bow and arrow? Who is he, with eyes full of tears, and steps that fear no one?

C And Aurash climbs further and further, no words on his lips, but a thousand thoughts in his head.

D The rocks moan under his feet: "Aurash, you've been destroyed. Can you ever return? Why did you choose to fight this battle?"

Scene Fourteen

C In the valley, whispers are heard in the dust. A corporal rushes in and throws himself before the Commander.

D (*as CORPORAL #2*) My lord, I've heard a terrible thing.

B Speak.

D It is not just, my lord. Our men have sworn that as soon as Aurash returns they will tear him apart joint from joint.

B And I won't stop them.

D Did I hear you well? Have we finished fighting the enemy so we can tear ourselves to pieces?

B Is this not fit for a traitor?

D Yes... but their King, that lunatic, will draw a sea of blood if we kill Aurash.

B He will protect Aurash until the arrow is released, but when he has what he wants, he'll forget Aurash ever existed.

<u>Scene Fifteen</u>

A Now, through the mist on the mountainside, a shadow looms, like the moon in front of the sun. *(as AURASH)* Father, why didn't you teach me how to cry?

C *(as the GHOST of AURASH's father)* I am the one who should cry.

A Have you heard it too, Father? You don't know me anymore, do you? It's not surprising, because I don't know Aurash myself.

C Everyone has abandoned you, Aurash. You are alone.

A I am full of spite.

C For your enemies?

A For my friends.

C Aurash, is it true that you have conspired with the enemy? Is that true?

A How can I convince you of anything else?

C I am not the one who must believe you: look down to the meadows, to all those people standing side by side. There is only you now, Aurash. The arrow: release it with your heart, not your arm.

A Isn't it useless?

C Useless?

A The horizon is so far.

C Throw it further.

A As far as the meadow that was once our home?

C Further.

A As far as the enemy's home?

C Further.

A To the eastern shores?

C Further.

A Beyond that?

C Further.

A Father, teach me to love.

C No.

A Give me strength.

C No. If you are full of spite, I have nothing left to give you: you are stronger than I. Listen, Aurash, your heart must release the arrow, not your arm.

D   So he said, and vanished.

Scene Sixteen

B   Here, a cave in the mountainside. Inside, the watchmen of the enemy, with blades of bronze and iron. One of the men approaches, a bird in his hands, and laughs.

C   *(as the ENEMY WATCHMAN #1)* Aurash, if that's you, tell us – who were you shouting at in the heart of the mountain? We looked and there was no one but you.

A   No one?

D   *(as the ENEMY WATCHMAN #2)* No one.

B   There was a distant cry, echoes, like the muffled screams of a wounded man. But we only saw you. *(as a STORYTELLER)* And the watchman releases the bird, a message tied to its tail.

A   Aurash climbs. He sees the mountain's wooden coat fall beneath the mist, further and further. Now a shield descends. Behind it, a man. He shouts:

C   *(as the FINAL WATCHMAN)* Aurash, take a good look at us: we are the watchmen of the fifth and final tower. We're the last men you'll ever see. On your way back, don't forget to tell us how you fired the arrow from that icy mountain peak.

D   Aurash climbs higher. He sees the watchman's tower slowly disappear. He hears nothing now, except the sound of his footsteps on the shoulder of the mountain. He climbs, and the joints in his body burn. He remembers his father told him once that when a scorpion is trapped in a fire, it stings itself and dies. And he, Aurash, sees himself trapped in the fire of his own thoughts.

Scene Seventeen

B   Then he stops: the smell of grass and dampness brings him to his senses. He looks around and sees that he too has been swallowed by the mist. His bow in both hands, he listens, like a tiger. A man appears, immense as an old tree, his hair white, as though winter snow had set upon his boughs. He comes forth with flaming eyes, and the fire on his tongue leaps out at Aurash.

C   *(as KASHVAD)* Don't be their only hope, Aurash!

D   Aurash recognizes Kashvad but says:

A   I don't know you.

C   Every treaty is broken one day. There will be troubles ahead. Where will you be then? Listen, Aurash, if you save your people now you will always be their hope in the future: the hope that in hard times a man will come to deliver them. In any crisis they will turn their eyes from themselves to find a chosen one. They will be weak, helpless.

A   His words are like an axe that hits the roots.

C   Your arrow releases them once, Aurash, but enslaves them forever.

D   Aurash turns around and looks at the peak of the mountain, which waits patiently for him. And when he turns back, Kashvad, too, has disappeared into the mist.

B   And he, Aurash, goes his way, higher. He listens to the playful winds, to the whispering earth; he hears his name called – twice, three times. He climbs and climbs and hears no sound at all, except for a cry, a hidden cry, beating deep within his chest.

Scene Eighteen

D   The mountain, that tall mountain, the Elborz, speaks to Aurash: *(as the ELBORZ mountain)* Aurash, will it so and I will pour a deadly flood upon your foes. If you desire it, I can make such lightning that everything will turn to ash. But tell me, Aurash, where are you off to so quickly? You are reaching the highest of the highs, the playground of the gods where no man is allowed to go.

B   And Aurash, who hears everything, says nothing. He goes on toward the highest of the highs, toward the playground of the gods. He climbs, with his curved bow and his arrow, the sky under his feet; the sky, the keeper of the clouds; the clouds, the vessel of the rain; the rain, the joy of the earth; and the earth below, full of grief. And he, Aurash, son of the grieving earth, reaches the highest of the highs.

Scene Nineteen

A   Mother Earth, this arrow belongs to Aurash, who was once a shepherd. Love has given him a passionate heart. He has never held a bow or released an arrow. He has never hurt an ant or set a trap. Who is Aurash? – who was unknown at dawn, and now at sunset has the eyes of the world upon him. He was a warrior whose most dangerous weapon was his shepherd's crook. Who is Aurash? – an ignorant farmer who won't even curse a man who steals from him. Who is Aurash? – a curved back that has been loaded and loaded but never complained. I am Aurash, a man once devout and pious. I was taught only to love: I turned my back on spite. But now there are scorpions in my head; now a man, a wicked man called Aurash has stained me with disgrace. He is

Aurash, standing on the other side of the earth, on the peak of a mountain, like a mirror, facing me, and his heart is my arrow's aim. He is a man so wretched, so disgraced, that he was condemned before he was tried. I am Aurash, the one who at sunrise was ignorant, and now, at sunset, knows something about the world. And he, Aurash screams: "I wish I didn't know!"

B   Aurash is frightened by his own cry. In front of a silent endless sky, he trembles.

A   I have left the earth but the earth refuses to let me go. Mother Earth, I have come to take refuge in you. You are the only one who knows me, who I am. Be my witness.

D   Then he, Aurash, the one to whom love gave a passionate heart, held his bow high, a bow that was more curved than the back of the sky.

Scene Twenty

B   The earth rose up: the sky crashed down. And Aurash with his feet on the earth and his face to the sky, placed his arrow in the bow.

C   He held it high, very high, and stood like a mountain.

D   He strung the bow and the clouds started to part.

C   He, Aurash, the son of the earth, drew the bow with all the might of his heart, and lightning cracked the sky.

B   His bow curved and curved further and further, and the waves of the sea retreated.

C   His bow curved more and more and the earth buckled.

B   The Elborz roared:

D   "How can I bear this weight on my shoulders?"

C   And the swift sun stopped moving, the earth's crust gave way, and the heavens turned redder than wine.

    The arrow is released.

A loud cry rose from the world, for on that highest of the highs, Aurash had disappeared.

B   And his arrow was travelling, and the people were shouting "Aurash will return, Aurash will return," and the arrow was flying with the wind in pursuit.

    Music. A celebration.

C   Horsemen who chased it, friends and foes, watched it disappear over the edge of the earth.

D The arrow flew, the wind at its tail, crossing deserts empty of life and green meadows where small huts grew tall.

A It flew over three mountains, seven vast plains, and five blue seas – one sea to the next and then onward to the other.

B Past the skies where the sun drives his chariot, and over seas where Venus comes walking.

Music. Celebration.

C The sun set three times, a storm struck and subsided three times, and the people waited three days on the slope of the Elborz for Aurash to return, but he didn't appear.

D And again for seven days, and he didn't return.

A How could he?

B He had released the arrow with his heart.

Music. Celebration.

C The arrow flew, followed by the wind.

D The arrow flew day after day, and night after night.

A Slaves and beggars saw it flash across the sky.

B Travellers on the roads couldn't believe their eyes.

C Everyone talked about it – father to daughter, brother to sister and wife to husband.

D Men who went in search of Aurash came back with wrinkled faces and white hair.

C And the arrow went on and on, from heart to heart, tribe to tribe, and generation to generation.

D And since that time, the arrow has been in flight.

Scene Twenty-one

Music.

A The sun offers its light to the sky and the earth.

B The dawn is beautiful.

C The clouds have shed soft tears.

D The meadows are green.

B There is peace.

C   There is joy.

A   The Elborz is high,

B   And her peak caresses the sky.

C   We are standing on her slope,

D   And in front of us, we see ourselves,

A   Our foes, our own blood, looking back at us with our own ghoulish smiles.
And I know many who still say: "Aurash will return,

D   Aurash will return,

C   Aurash will return,

B   Aurash will return."

The end.

The Death
of the King

Bahram Beyza'ie
Translated by Soheil Parsa with Peter Farbridge

Peter James, Tanja Jacobs
photographer unknown

The Death of the King was first produced by Modern Times Stage Company at W Space, Toronto, from April 3 to April 24, 1994 with the following company:

MILLER	Peter James
GIRL	Tracy Wright
WOMAN	Tanja Jacobs
CHIEF COMMANDER	Andrew Scorer
MAGU	Stan Coles
PRIVATE	Duncan Ward
CORPORAL	Dean Marshall

Direction: Soheil Parsa
Lighting Design: Aisling Sampson
Set Design: Gita Hashemi & Soheil Parsa
Costume Design: Gita Hashemi
Stage Manager: Joanne Fishburn
Producer: George Mirabelli

· · ·

Awards & Nominations
Dora Mavor Moore Awards: Outstanding New Play–Translation and Adaptation (Soheil Parsa and Peter Farbridge). Dora Mavor Moore Nominations: Outstanding Performance by a Female (Tracy Wright), Outstanding Costume Design (Gita Hashemi), Outstanding Set Design (Gita Hashemi & Soheil Parsa), Outstanding Direction of a Play (Soheil Parsa).

Characters

MILLER
GIRL
WOMAN
CHIEF COMMANDER
MAGU
PRIVATE
CORPORAL

Translator's Foreword

"Yazdgird fled to Merv where he was killed by a miller for sake of his gold and armour."

—*Avesta: The Religious Book of the Parsees*, A.H. Bleeck

History

Around the middle of the seventh century CE, Persia faced ten years of onslaughts from a fearless and religiously impassioned Moslem army. It was a ruthless and brutal invasion, one which would spell the end of the opulent Persian Empire.

The reigning monarch at the time was King Yazdgird III, the last of the Sasanian kings. Yazdgird rushed from city to city, hiding from the invaders and vainly attempting to solicit help from neighbouring countries. His final stop was a mill in the city of Merv.

The year is 642 CE.

But for Bahram Beyza'i, the death of this King takes place in the year "zero," when one epoch had ended and another had just begun. History wrote the roles of the Miller and the King. Beyza'i has recast them.

The Death of the King [1]

The interior of a mill. Dimly lit and in ruins. On the floor by the millstone, there is a dead man. A priest kneels in prayer over him, burning incense. A MILLER stands with his face frozen in terror. His wife stands. His daughter screams.

MILLER   No! My lords, nobles, generals, armed from head to toe – this is not right – or anything – it's a terrible mistake. Yes, the blood of this trespasser was spilt here, but I'm not guilty of this. He wanted to die. No! Officers, Oh knights, such armour – this – what you're doing is – we don't deserve—

CHIEF COMMANDER   Miller! Your arms are steeped in blood to the elbows. Our sentence is as follows. You shall all be executed at once, but not all at once – you, Miller, will be hung, just short of death, your limbs will be torn off and your bones pounded before your eyes – your wife shall be burnt to cinders in your oven, and your daughter – her skin will be slit open crown to navel and the wound stuffed with straw. A notice of your godless crime will be hung on every farmer's gate across the land. Thus will the name of the Miller remain defiled until the end of time.

MAGU   May Daevas be destroyed be destroyed be destroyed the Daevas. May blackness be expelled be expelled be expelled the blackness. Let light come from the shadow. Let the fire burn smokeless. Let the light be not smothered. May Daevas be destroyed be destroyed be destroyed the Daevas. May blackness be expelled be expelled be expelled the blackness…

PRIVATE   We'll need some wood and rope. Where do you keep the wood around here?

WOMAN   Shameless man! Is this an execution or a robbery?

CHIEF COMMANDER   Just tear a beam out of the barn. That should bear the weight.

WOMAN   Yes, hurry up! God forbid that we should live. God forbid the truth be strewn about the country so everyone can mock this, our glorious King. Yes, please hurry.

PRIVATE   Let me finish them off right now. *(raising his sword)* One wave of my sword. Two on the down stroke, one on the way up!

CHIEF COMMANDER   *(stopping him)* We want justice, not butchery. They will not be killed for killing's sake. They will die for having drained the sea from our King's fathomless heart. He, the leader of all leaders, the King of all kings. King Yazdgird the Third, son of the son of the first King Yazdgird. That river of blood there in the dust once flowed blue in the four hundred and sixty-six veins of

---

[1] The original title in Farsi translates as *The Death of Yazdgird*.

this champion. Through the head of this man the conscience of God spoke to his body, the people. In these dark times, what greater service could one give our enemy than to sever the head from the body?

MAGU   When the millennium ends, the Age of the Lamb will be over, the Time of the Wolf will begin and Daevas will dance on the corpses of angels.

GIRL   The King's not dead! The King's not dead!

CHIEF COMMANDER   *(pointing to the corpse)* What's this then?

GIRL   Him? He sleeps and dreams we are here.

MILLER   Don't be an idiot, girl. Do you want them to mock us?

CHIEF COMMANDER   He was gathering a massive army. It could have rid this land of that scourge out there.

CORPORAL   All hope is lost now.

> *The PRIVATE exits.*

WOMAN   No, no, we didn't kill him! You can't condemn us for something that didn't happen!

CHIEF COMMANDER   Lies. Corporal, you saw them, didn't you, the King dead at their feet?

CORPORAL   Yes, I was the first to step foot into this devastation, and what I saw made my heart stop cold. In the darkness I could see the millstone, frozen still, as if perhaps it had never ever spun before – and these three were there, weeping over the body of the King. He looked more glorious than I had ever seen him, lying in his royal gowns. From up above, up there – a shaft of light cut across the gloom and fell upon his face. The dust. Swirling up. Like a thousand angels captured in the beam. Yes, I saw it all, and it will stay with me 'til the day I die. The blood running under the millstone. Shadows of death hiding in every corner. But what astonished me the most was how these stone-hearted creatures could weep and wail over their own quarry.

MILLER   No, not for him, but for ourselves we wept.

WOMAN   *(She moans.)* For a son...

GIRL   *(through tears)* My brother...

WOMAN   I nursed him, from a babe to sturdy boy, I nursed him with every drop of my blood. My only son. And your vermin took him to fight. And before the new moon had come, they brought me home his bloody corpse, eight lances thrusting from his back.

MAGU   Do you consider that young boy to be the same value as our King?

WOMAN   Heavens, did I say so? No, my son was not as valuable as the King – he was much more precious to me.

CHIEF COMMANDER   Did you hear that? This is why Persia is crumbling. I see it now, Miller. You were seeking to avenge the death of your son on the King.

MILLER   It's true, my heart was full of hate... but all the same I didn't kill him. Not from any goodness in me, but from fear.

WOMAN   You said "All kings have guards – they will come for him."

MILLER   As you see I wasn't wrong.

WOMAN   You said "God stop me from hurting him."

MILLER   And I did not.

GIRL   Our chief witness, he's nodded off.

MAGU   Lies! I won't tolerate this. You have ground the blood of the divine's shadow under your millstone and now your own tin cups shall brim red and your bones will crack between the jaws of wolves. This is the immutable word. Your household will be annihilated.

MILLER   *(to himself)* Now I feel the wind is on its way. In the eye of this storm they wind my noose, pitch my gallows. Their swords thirst for blood – soon they will be satisfied. All my pleas bounce back at me like arrows from a shield. *(to the King's men)* Oh my warriors, I will pay for my crimes, yes – but for the crime of poverty – no other sin than that.

MAGU   You will pay penance for the sin of avarice. Tell us. What were you after? His armour? The golden breastplate? His bronze leg-guards? It's obvious. Every inferior wishes to rise above his superior. The gasping runner who lags behind the pack wants nothing more than to outpace the leader. What is the dream of the defeated? Victory. The man on foot envies the horsebound. The beggar is rival to the king.

MILLER   But in spite of this I didn't kill him. Not from lack of need, but from fear.

WOMAN   You said "All kings have escorts – they will race after him."

MILLER   I was a fool, I was afraid.

WOMAN   You said "I will never hit him."

MILLER   And I did not.

GIRL   Our chief witness, he's nodded off.

   The PRIVATE enters.

PRIVATE   I got the wood from the barn. It should bear the Miller's weight.

The PRIVATE exits.

GIRL *(running to her mother's arms)* If Father dies I'll be even lonelier!

WOMAN *(pulling away)* Lonelier? Don't worry my sweet – you too will soon be dead, with me by your side. *(to herself)* Now the enemy is whirling in from all sides like a wind with eight faces. From mountainside, forest and field, from ocean, river, hill and valley – they are coming. Here, in the eye of the storm, I am alone. *(yelling at the King's men)* Find the King's murderers, yes! But not in here, out there! Whatever king he was, he was murdered all by himself – the man who came in here was a weakling.

CHIEF COMMANDER Hold your tongue!

WOMAN No! If I can't say this now, when can I? From my grave? The King wasn't murdered here – he was dead long before he came to us.

CHIEF COMMANDER *(to the MILLER)* Shut that woman up! *(to the WOMAN)* Did not a man, lost in a storm, come here?

WOMAN He came like a shadow, searching for death in a dark corner.

CHIEF COMMANDER Stop this nonsense! *(to the MILLER)* Speak or be whipped. Did not a man of great bearing, dressed in the garments of a king, come here?

MILLER When I see him now, coming down the hill to my front door, I wish I could pluck out my eyes with my own fingers.

CHIEF COMMANDER Then he did come to this place?

MILLER Yes.

CHIEF COMMANDER On his own two feet?

MILLER Yes, yes. He was terrified. He came in rags.

CHIEF COMMANDER You're talking about the King of kings!

MILLER How were we supposed to know? He came in like a criminal, and to this place too, no more than a cave. He was so afraid we thought he was a thief running from the law.

WOMAN He fell into a corner and said – "Shut the windows!"

MILLER *(to the GIRL)* And your heart froze, didn't it?

WOMAN No doubt he was a thief.

MILLER Or a beggar. How could we know?

GIRL Give me something to eat.

CHIEF COMMANDER   All right speak then. While they're building your gallows. Tell us what the King told you. Was he preparing a new offensive on the invaders?

GIRL   He said "Give me something to eat."

MILLER   Something to eat? Here.

GIRL   Stale bread?

MILLER   We could make you some fresh.

GIRL   Meat. I'm hungry. Give me some meat.

WOMAN   Meat? Did you hear what he said?

GIRL   What? You don't eat meat here? You have never seen a quail or a pheasant before? There's not a single lamb or goat to exchange for a coin?

MILLER   We'd be lucky to have a goat. The milk could cure our daughter's sickness.

GIRL   I am hungry and you are thinking about elixirs for that whelp? What have I stumbled into? What quality of people are you? Who would believe that beyond the walls of the Palace of the Kings there are such beasts? Neither angels of the fire nor worshippers of the flame.

MILLER   The Palace? Did you hear that, wife? Everything I mill goes there.

GIRL   I'm hungry.

WOMAN   Why didn't you stay in the Palace of the Kings? You wouldn't be starving now.

GIRL   How do you expect me to eat stale barley bread?

WOMAN   You moisten it. For guests we add a bit of cheese.

GIRL   *(whimpering, as herself)* He ate my dinner. *(as the King)* Shut your face, you little bitch! Fetch me some water.

WOMAN   He's ordering us in our own house.

MILLER   This man doesn't seem like a beggar. Beggars beg – he commands.

WOMAN   Whoever he is, by the looks of the glint coming from his bag, has as much money as might. We have to get a look in it.

MILLER   Be patient. Wait 'til he's sleeping. There is a typhoon out there...

CHIEF COMMANDER   So when he was asleep you pilfered through his bag.

WOMAN   But when we found the pearls we were sure he had robbed a king.

MAGU   The imperial pearls should have instructed you that he was the King.

MILLER   Would a king run away? Beg like a pauper? Steal his own treasure like a thief? Hide himself in rags? We saw the velvet robes he had stashed away, and that golden crown – we thought he had robbed a king.

GIRL   *(laughing, as the King)* Such a feast. *(crying, as herself)* The King isn't dead! *(yelling, as the King)* The allies have deserted! The invaders are everywhere! Retreat! Retreat!

CHIEF COMMANDER   Damnation! We were so close. Our horses were almost on top of him, but then the wind – we fell behind and lost him in the storm. Darkness snatched our reins and led us astray.

MAGU   A curse upon the evil deeds of Ahriman. Once, twice, thrice and thirty times.

CHIEF COMMANDER   In the gloom before the dawn, when sky was folded like the wings of a raven, our faithful steeds broke their ropes, flew off into the darkness. We finally found them at this mill. And when we opened the door, we saw the King's gashes, fountains of blood reddening the horizon.

GIRL   *(smiling)* Girls understand the colour of blood.

WOMAN   Shut up! You don't fear the back of my hand?

GIRL   Fear? Have I something more to lose?

CORPORAL   *(drawing his sword)* His blood. It shines like the midnight sun.

MAGU   His gashes are thirsting for justice.

CORPORAL   They must die!

CHIEF COMMANDER   Stop! Would you have them die with one blow? I'm sure they would like it that way – painless, quick. No, I have other plans. They will be slowly drained of life. Step by step – they will languish.

CORPORAL   Pray, Magu, pray.

MAGU   How does the moon wax? How does she wane? Who other than thou, divine, can cause her to wax and wane? Come, may You save us. Come, may You soothe us. Come, may You absolve us. May You come see our triumph.

MILLER   Who will pray for our dead?

MAGU   Die! I forswear you, impious ones. Die! I rebuke you, evildoers. Die! I abjure you, unbelievers. May Ahriman's followers be destroyed. May we never follow him, may we never reach his threshold, may we never serve his design.

CORPORAL   Isn't there some prayer that could wake him from death?

MAGU   How can one be woken from death, my son?

CORPORAL   I know… I know…

MILLER   But he did wake up. Remember? He woke up.

GIRL   He was tossing and turning.

WOMAN   Drop the bag.

MILLER   He woke with a growl. He reached one hand under his head.

WOMAN   He reached one hand under his head for his bag of gold and his other hand for the hilt of his sword.

GIRL   *(as the King)* You! What are you doing with that?

MILLER   When he found out we knew about his treasure, he jumped up and roared, "I am the King! Look at me! I am the King!" *(to the WOMAN)* You laughed.

GIRL   She laughed. *(The WOMAN is laughing.)*

MILLER   *(as the King)* I am the King.

WOMAN   *(stops laughing)* Everyone is a king in his own house. The king of this ditch is the Miller.

MILLER   He drew his sword.

GIRL   He drew his sword.

WOMAN   If you're such a hero why don't you go off and fight the invaders? Why bring this bravado in here?

MILLER   Oh my head!

GIRL   He held his head in his hands.

MILLER   There are a thousand drums pounding. There is an army in there greater than the sand of the Sahara.

WOMAN   He's trying to fool us.

GIRL   You're right. He doesn't act like a king.

MAGU   It's him, it's him by God! I know those robes, that golden armour, that breastplate, the leg-guards – yes, I know the King when I see him.

WOMAN   He was terrified, hysterical, he was inconsolable. He was moaning, hitting his head on the wall. He whined about how his enemies were coming. He wanted to hide the sword and the crown, to hide himself.

MILLER   I raged at him.

WOMAN   He raged.

MILLER   I insulted him.

WOMAN   *(anxiously)* No, you didn't.

MILLER "My King, O Ruler," I said, "who is responsible for all my suffering. I've paid you taxes every single day of my life, I've fed your soldiers, and now the enemy is coming you're running away and leaving me? Me? Who knows nothing about war, and has no strength left to fight?" Yes, I raged at him. I hit him.

WOMAN You hit him.

MILLER Once, twice. Yes! Three times.

CHIEF COMMANDER And your hand didn't break? You struck him and the sky didn't collapse?

MILLER I hit him.

WOMAN We never believed he was a king. He looked more like a filthy crook.

MAGU Be quiet! Don't you know that the soul of the dead rests beside the pillow of its body for three days and nights? He's here, among us. Do not disturb him. Do not anger him.

MILLER You mean the soul of the King is still here? *(to the WOMAN)* Did you hear that?

> The MILLER and the WOMAN begin scurrying around the mill.

WOMAN Get it! Block the doors! Don't let it get away!

MILLER Beat it! Hit it! Get it!

CHIEF COMMANDER What in God's name are you doing?

MILLER Go to hell, soul, or speak up and tell them the truth!

WOMAN Speak, soul, where are you hiding?

MILLER Where are you? Over there? Get it!

WOMAN You brought these thugs here, so you answer to them.

MAGU Stop! Stop this blasphemy! You look like the worshippers of Ahriman. Have you renounced your faith?

WOMAN If you can't stand to listen then plug your ears, because I'm thinking of the worst language possible.

CHIEF COMMANDER I won't allow the soul of our King to be blasphemed in this way.

CORPORAL Do you hear? These nobles won't tolerate your dirty language.

WOMAN Are swear words just more jewels in your nobles' coffers that they can pick out and spend at will? No, they're rocks, piles of shit I find on the ground and I can chuck them at you.

CHIEF COMMANDER You have added the hot iron spike to your sentence.

WOMAN   Is that the best you can do?

CORPORAL   Your tongue will be cut off, woman.

GIRL   *(crying)* Don't provoke them.

WOMAN   Why not? *(to the CORPORAL)* But my tongue knows secrets about your King. Did I tell you he had a nightmare?

MAGU   A dream?

WOMAN   Yes. Something people see when they're sleeping.

MAGU   Is it true? Our King had a nightmare? Everyone agrees that there are secrets in these dreams. Tell us about his vision.

> *The PRIVATE enters.*

PRIVATE   Good news, Commander. Fortune's with us. Our scouts have captured one of the invaders. He's bleeding, half-dead.

CORPORAL   One of the invaders?

PRIVATE   He looks just like us, only different somehow. He speaks our tongue, but I can't understand it. And his flag – it's like our flag, only it's been painted black.

CORPORAL   What has he told us so far?

CHIEF COMMANDER   What we need to know is what he hasn't told us.

CORPORAL   What kind of man is he? Foot soldier, drummer or stableman?

PRIVATE   He's a lost man.

CHIEF COMMANDER   Every man is lost unto himself. What kind of man is he?

PRIVATE   He's just a man, hungry and stubborn.

CHIEF COMMANDER   Then give him some bread and whip him 'til he speaks. Is he a messenger or spy? We must know how many troops there are, where they are and what they're up to. Are they riding or on foot? Near or far? Why do they burn and destroy everything? Why do they wear black? And the God they speak of – why is he so angry?

PRIVATE   He won't answer, Commander.

CHIEF COMMANDER   Why not? He refuses to talk?

PRIVATE   He can't speak our language.

CHIEF COMMANDER   Well tie him to a tree and beat him 'til he does! Are the gallows ready?

PRIVATE   Everything but the oven to heat the spike.

GIRL   *(covering her eyes)* Oh!

MILLER *(happy)* We've run out of coal...

CHIEF COMMANDER Don't get your hopes up. If we can't make a fire then we'll stick cold spikes in your eyes.

> *The PRIVATE exits.*

MAGU You said the King had a dream.

WOMAN Yes, he had a dream – a king's dream.

MAGU Was there a message in it? Why did he wake up so frightened?

WOMAN He was afraid of you.

CHIEF COMMANDER Afraid of us?

WOMAN Of people like you.

CHIEF COMMANDER That tongue of yours will cut off your head!

WOMAN If my tongue can't free my head then let it cut it off.

MILLER *(pleading with her)* What can you get by arguing?

WOMAN What can I lose?

CHIEF COMMANDER Tell us about the dream.

WOMAN No.

MAGU Tell us. It's the Chief Commander's order.

WOMAN My tongue has been ordered cut off. It's not easy for a tongueless person to speak.

CORPORAL The high priest is asking politely. What do you want us to do – get on our knees?

WOMAN You don't have much choice.

GIRL Don't frighten me!

MILLER Don't make things worse!

WOMAN Don't come closer!

CORPORAL Please!

WOMAN *(as the King)* I'm thirsty.

MAGU Water!

WOMAN Throw it away! *(to the GIRL)* Build a fire. It's like a dungeon in here – I can't see a thing. Is there no light anywhere?

MAGU What's happened to him?

CORPORAL Have you ever seen him like this?

GIRL   Why is he so scared?

MILLER   What's he hiding from?

WOMAN   Light!

GIRL   What's the matter?

WOMAN   I've had a nightmare. Where are my dream interpreters?

MAGU   I'm here, Majesty.

WOMAN   In my dream, I was galloping across an endless moor. The ground was not thistles, not grass, but daggers and swords.

MILLER   My entire life has been a nightmare. What else could one expect in this crumbling mill, my ancestor's ruins, but a nightmare.

WOMAN   Misfortune swept down on me, her wings made of wind.

MAGU   A dream that comes when it is neither dark nor bright and when day vanquishes the night, always has a message.

WOMAN   And there, on a white Nisaean steed – that man, that hero, forefather of my heart, that warrior whose very look mortified his enemy – the Mighty Hunter, Bahram Gur. He led me forth, bearing his standard high before him. But then a wind rose up, a dark wind, like a Daevas' scorching breath, and a hundred hundred whistling hooves hurled sand into my eyes. And when I opened them, he was gone – the fire of the storm had consumed him. (*She offers the MILLER a club.*)

CORPORAL   So that's why he was so afraid.

WOMAN   My troops, that rabble of traitors – when I, armed with their pledges, battered my way to the enemy, they turned their backs on me and fled. I had not one grey hair before that day, but then solitude gripped my heart so tightly that all the colour ran from the tips. So great was my terror that the enemy, seeing me come, split asunder and made the way open to me.

MILLER   Did you hear that? He ran away from his friends, not his enemies.

WOMAN   What became of good thoughts, good words, good deeds? Who blackened our sacred standard? Oh! Stones are hailing down on me!

GIRL   Listen to that! He really is a king.

WOMAN   A king with fright for a flag and loneliness for troops.

MILLER   You shouldn't have told me that you're the King. There is a great pain in my heart… I had a son once—

WOMAN   Don't!

MILLER   He was forced into your army, and when he returned... (*He takes the club.*)

WOMAN   My son...

GIRL   My brother... (*The MILLER raises the club.*)

WOMAN   (*to the MILLER*) Do it!

MILLER   No. All kings have guards. They will come for him. (*He lowers the club.*)

WOMAN   My son, my son...

MILLER   The clouds are pressing down on me. I hear the wind howling now. The storm is wrapping around us.

CHIEF COMMANDER   These rabble think of nothing but themselves – these people of common birth – forever scrounging in the muck, sniffing out their next mouthful of water, their next crust of bread. What could the King find here? Baseness. Savagery. These—

WOMAN   You snake! Scorpion mouth! Oh, such highbrowed birth! I know you very well – pretenders! Fakes! You false nobles exploit us, then punish us because you were able to. But the only difference between you and me is that sword on your hip.

CHIEF COMMANDER   Your tongue will be cut out, woman.

WOMAN   Well there has to be some reason for that sword.

GIRL   (*to herself*) If there were any flour, I'd pour it on my head. Then maybe Venus would step down from the sun, take me for her daughter, and bathe me in a stream.

WOMAN   My husband is a miller – a man who has done nothing with his life but grind misery under a stone – a man who in winter and summer made only sighs and sweat. This is my husband, to whom you have promised your swords. What do we have except a roof that wants to crush us and a growling millstone chasing its tail?

> *The GIRL laughs.*

MILLER   Silence! Can't you hear that scraping? I've heard that in the Palace of a Hundred Pillars, the ancient stone faces have all uprooted themselves – abandoned a thousand years of tributes to take refuge in the wilderness.

GIRL   I laughed at you.

MILLER   I laughed too, once upon a time.

CHIEF COMMANDER   (*to the MILLER*) Take his crown and put it on. Tell us what the King told you.

WOMAN   (*dressing the MILLER*) His forehead was furrowed with thoughts. He hit himself. He brooded…

MILLER   My horse abandoned me not far from this place. She threw me down and melted into the wind. The dead are rising from their tombs. Lightning is falling on the people. They say my subjects are welcoming the enemy with dates and bread.

CHIEF COMMANDER   He's talking like the King.

MILLER   What do sages say about kings who are fugitives in their own land?

WOMAN   Not much.

MILLER   I am a fugitive in this land. I run from house to house, but there are no tables laid for me, no beds with their sheets turned down. The people have all gone. Shame comes to me. Rather than take me into combat, even my most trusted horses lead me away.

WOMAN   Don't try to fool us. You're carrying on like this so we won't ask you how you got your hands on this gold. The truth is you are a man just like my husband – poor and dirty. I'll forgive you the money for your bread if you'll get out of here now.

MILLER   With what horse? To where? The gates of the world have shut in my face.

WOMAN   Yes, and this is the only place you found, like some beggar's hostel that never closes. I've asked this miller a hundred times to fix the bolt, but he wouldn't listen to me.

MILLER   The sun and the moon have risen together. I'm not safe anywhere. (*The GIRL moans.*) What are you whining about?

GIRL   My chest, my stomach – they hurt.

MILLER   It is hunger, girl – I too have discovered what this feels like. In the Palace of the Kings, I heard nothing of the outside. I couldn't hear the moans. I turned my back on the world and now the world has turned its back on me. (*The GIRL moans.*) What are you whining about?

GIRL   My pains.

MILLER   Yes, you told me before. Why did I forget? In my palace I locked the doors one by one behind me. Here the locks are broken. I must have your mill. How much for it, Miller?

WOMAN   He wants us to put a price on this ruin.

MILLER   Put this sieve on your head, be the Miller, and tell me what I answered. Is there no one here who will exchange this ruin for some of my gold?

WOMAN   (*putting a sieve on her head*) There is no profit in this trade – we are bankrupt and helpless. The millstone has worn down, the spindles are broken, and we ate the mule long ago.

> *The GIRL moans.*

MILLER   What are you whining about?

GIRL   The heartache. There is no profit here except the wound in my chest left by this place.

MILLER   Take the money and be free.

WOMAN   Why does he want to part with his gold? (*to the MILLER*) These days, being the master of gold is a pain in the neck – someone with money is never safe. (*to the King*) There are people out there, aren't there, waiting to ambush you, and we'll be your stooges.

MILLER   (*holding up the bag of gold*) Count them.

WOMAN   Stolen gold.

GIRL   He's not a thief. What sort of thief would spend his money on this?

WOMAN   Why do you need this old ruin? The roof is collapsing, and all the neighbours have fled. If you don't want it to mill, what do you need it for?

MILLER   To kill myself.

ALL   To kill yourself?

WOMAN   That's what he said.

MILLER   To kill myself.

WOMAN   How much?

MILLER   Half of everything.

WOMAN   This is some sort of sick game. You'll grant us a second of hope, snatch it away, then laugh at our suffering.

MILLER   It is the world that is laughing at me. I'll give you all the gold.

WOMAN   Done.

MILLER   On one condition.

WOMAN   I knew it. All right, what is it?

MILLER   My hand – it will not obey me.

WOMAN   You're afraid?

MILLER   The dagger will not obey me.

CHIEF COMMANDER   Kings do not fear death! Kings are not immortal, but they have no fear of death!

GIRL   You dread death as much as life.

MILLER   In every joint of my body.

MAGU   He, the King, said he was afraid?

WOMAN   In all his four hundred and sixty-six blue veins.

CHIEF COMMANDER   I don't want to hear this. I won't listen.

CORPORAL   In the army of liars you are the commander. I won't take this from you. Did the King himself say that he was afraid?

WOMAN   Tell me, King, I couldn't quite hear you properly. You said you were scared?

MILLER   In the very marrow of my bones.

CHIEF COMMANDER   Cursed be our fate.

MILLER   I will give you all the gold if you help me.

WOMAN   What do you mean "help"?

MILLER   You must stab me…

CHIEF COMMANDER   Do you hear this? The Miller is trying to clear his name.

MILLER   …so that I don't know when or from where it is coming – do it suddenly, from behind, or while I am asleep—any way you like—just don't let me know when.

WOMAN   This is murder, not help.

MILLER   My bag is full of coins— *(as the MILLER)* Tell them what I said.

WOMAN   The Miller said, "I'm beginning to see what it is to be a king. But if it's so terrible, why do soldier and noble risk their life to become one."

MILLER   My enemies are thirsting for my blood. I'm so sick of life. If only I had my horse.

WOMAN   To be honest, I'd like to see his head on a stake, too – my days wouldn't have been so miserable if he'd been a better king. But I'm a man whose hands are clean – I've milled my bread with barley, but never with blood. Wife, help me – would this be a just act? *(as the WOMAN)* You, girl, come here, be the Miller's wife and tell them what I said.

GIRL   *(playfully)* Me, the Miller's wife? Oh Miller, hold me in your arms for just a minute more.

WOMAN   Shameless child! Just be the Miller's wife and listen to the King.

MILLER   I wish I could be free, a shepherd somewhere… everyone can escape except for a king.

GIRL   Kings and leaders run away every day and we are left in the hands of murderers.

MILLER   This time is not like the others. You cannot murder a nation, but a king – yes. And with a king's death comes the death of the nation.

WOMAN   What's that sound?

GIRL   The coins.

MILLER   A gold mine.

WOMAN   Can you hear that?

GIRL   I could have used that gold the day my son's freedom was for sale, or my daughter's medicine. But now I'm stranded in a desert barren of life – gold has no value here.

MILLER   There will come an end to this suffering. The people will return, the ruins will be rebuilt, and these houses filled with children. You will be happy again.

WOMAN   Happy? Among the invaders?

MILLER   Such has been the course of history since history was. Just hide your treasure and no one will know.

WOMAN   *(to the GIRL)* Are you listening, wife? It makes me wonder. Would we be found out? Would our well run red with his blood?

GIRL   Why are you asking me when you already have the answer? Are you really that blind? He's testing our loyalty, our devotion to him. As soon as you take the gold, that smouldering in his eyes will burst into flames and scorch the lot of us. Refuse the gold, pretend you are angry and flatter him with protests. If he is the King, maybe he'll throw you a few coins. Whatever the case, have you ever heard of a king that wants to die?

WOMAN   That's exactly what I was thinking. Yes, he's taken us for fools, and now he's testing us. No! Whoever you are, know this – I'm a miller, not a thief.

CHIEF COMMANDER   Now that he's gone, these lies all seem true.

WOMAN   My husband gave him a place to sleep, some bread and water.

MAGU   Is this a place for rest?

WOMAN   He gave him everything he had.

MAGU   Water in tin cups.

WOMAN   It's not our sin that they're cheap.

MAGU   Such hospitality!

WOMAN   The King asked him three times to kill him in return for his gold, and all three times he refused.

MAGU   That is hearsay. The King kill himself? If it be so, give us proof, indisputable proof.

CHIEF COMMANDER   Yes, proof!

CORPORAL   There's something burning inside me… yes… now that the world is tilting, I can say this without fear, in spite of my rank…

CHIEF COMMANDER   What's this about? The King or his assassins?

CORPORAL   We didn't lose him in the storm. It was he who fled from us.

MAGU   You accuse the shepherd of abandoning his sheep?

CORPORAL   Not his sheep, no, he ran away from misfortune. I saw him with my own eyes, strapping the saddle to his horse's back.

CHIEF COMMANDER   If you were not the soldier I know you to be, I would say you are the enemy.

CORPORAL   I saw him mount his bay. Secretly. I saw him—alone—putting his foot into the stirrup.

CHIEF COMMANDER   The King? Who always has a hundred hands outstretched to lift him? Now I know why you're still a corporal.

CORPORAL   If I'm wrong so be it, but tell me why.

CHIEF COMMANDER   Our King was lion-hearted, the rival of the dragon. Are you telling us that such a man took his life because a few tent dwellers crossed his path?

MILLER   He ordered me to do it.

GIRL   Say it!

MILLER   He ordered me.

WOMAN   *(covering her ears)* Never! Never!

MILLER   Four times.

WOMAN   Never! We will never kill a guest!

MILLER   Is there nothing written in the holy book about obeying a king's command?

MAGU   Of course there is, my lord. It's written that your words are God's divine words heard in earthly form.

MILLER   *(handing the WOMAN a knife)* The Divine command.

WOMAN   I won't obey it.

MILLER   He who refuses a king's order will be disgraced in death. The Daevas will break his body and he will live under the earth for nine thousand years of nightmares. Since my gold cannot seem to convince you, I will command you from my kingly position, high above your shoulders. I command you to kill me. Have you no fear?

WOMAN   If you are the King, your soldiers will come looking for you. It's them I fear.

MILLER   Has death turned her back on me, too?

WOMAN   You said that with your death the nation will die. How can I stain my hands with the blood of a nation?

GIRL   Kill him, man, and maybe with his death a new nation will be born.

WOMAN   I'm a miller, not a midwife. I give people bread, that's all. It's the only thing I know how to do.

MILLER   The world has chosen you to shed my blood. Ah, everyone, everything forsakes me. Except the invaders' troops – they cling to my back like a shadow.

WOMAN   Those troops are not your enemy. You created your enemy – your people's misery. Otherwise, how could the invaders walk through the country like this?

MAGU   Many of our temples are still standing. People must be taught the severity of combat under the kind rule of God.

WOMAN   Enough, Priest. We put our faith in you once, and what did we get in return?

CHIEF COMMANDER   We used to pull out the tongues of those who said such things.

WOMAN   Do you have any other talents besides the removal of tongues?

CORPORAL   (*beginning to leave*) I've changed my verdict.

CHIEF COMMANDER   (*stopping him*) Our verdict is final!

MILLER   You have been cast in your role, Miller. I command you one last time – take me to the feast of my blood.

GIRL   He said, "Rejecting a king's order is like doing battle with God."

MILLER   No one in this land can reject the King's order.

WOMAN   Really? Very nice. If that's so, then order the invaders' troops to get out of Persia.

MILLER   You mock me.

WOMAN   Your order was an order in the Palace of the Kings, not here.

MILLER   *(to the King's men)* Did you hear that? I refused.

CHIEF COMMANDER   Can a menial refuse a king's order?

WOMAN   I'm confused. If we kill him it will be murder, if we don't, it will be treason. What exactly should we do?

MILLER   Nothing, wife... this sin was born at the same time as I was – it is my soul's twin, whose name is poverty.

> *The PRIVATE enters.*

PRIVATE   The gallows are ready. Still looking for the rope.

CHIEF COMMANDER   The man hasn't talked yet?

PRIVATE   He'd spluttered something, but like I said, I don't get a word of it. Maybe you officers could understand. Do you want me to bring him in here?

CHIEF COMMANDER   No.

PRIVATE   *(to the WOMAN)* I said I need rope.

WOMAN   It's in the barn. Don't take all of it.

> *The PRIVATE exits.*

CORPORAL   Every time this country is overrun, the rich flee and the poor stay behind to be captured. Why didn't you escape too?

MILLER   There was no mule for the bags.

GIRL   The world hungers for my innocence. The curses of my life will be read out loud – the mule dies, the neighbours flee, the millstone breaks, and now this man brings death here.

MAGU   No. It's inconceivable that the Miller was not seduced by the gold. It's inconceivable that his hand didn't work the dagger. You were his assassin. Any other thought is inconceivable.

WOMAN   When our stranger was denied his death, he tried a different trick.

MILLER   He tried to provoke me.

GIRL   Why didn't you get angry?

MILLER   He stared at my face. Stared and stared and stared. *(The WOMAN spits at him.)*

GIRL   No! No! No!

> *The WOMAN hits the MILLER.*

Heart of stone!

WOMAN   You are a fool, a simpleton. For years in this desert you ground barley and dates. Don't you crave vengeance now? Am I not your King, your enemy? You haven't seen the Palace of the Kings, have you? I assure you we do not sleep on straw mats. You have not seen the imperial carpet – threads of silver and gold, woven into rivers, meadows and clouds. I have a chessboard with ruby and topaz squares, a backgammon table inlaid with blue-green emeralds. Shall I continue? The Bridal treasure, the Emperor's chest, the Athenian Necklace, the Throne of Solomen, and the Golden Harem with its bounty of twelve thousand slave girls. Need more? Is there not the power to hate inside you?

MILLER   I told him: "Oh man, rags, king or crook—whatever you are—don't try to provoke me."

WOMAN   Twelve hundred elephants, thirteen thousand camels, the Hunting Enclave, the Diamond Cave, twelve thousand hunting dogs, and seven hundred thousand horsemen, thirteen hundred thousand troops, six hundred thousand horses, and a hundred thousand swords in their scabbards. And every year, in tribute alone, I receive some two thousand thousand times a thousand gold coins.

MILLER   I told him, "Tyrant, don't try to drive me mad. I'm a man who's given up his share of years and today or tomorrow I may give up my life. Misery has made me cruel. Don't make me raise a hand to a guest."

WOMAN   He laughed. He took the whip and said "You don't even have the guts of a common hand-slave in you, man! Manure is clean compared to you. I'll have to teach you how to serve your King. Let's see… I have guard dogs I haven't heard for a long time. Crawl at my feet. Yelp! Whimper!

MILLER   *(falling to his knees)* Don't disgrace me. I warn you, I can't take this forever. Time has hardened my heart like a millstone, and if I strike it, my hand too will become as terrible. Leave me be. Let me go.

WOMAN   Get away from me! I have just noticed your daughter in the shadows. She is sick, yes, but still desirable. Her lips are red as cherries – ripe and aching to be picked. Take me to feast of her body's fruit.

MILLER   No, don't disgrace me more than this. I know you're just testing my loyalty but there's no questioning that. Let me kiss your feet, my King.

GIRL   He's on his knees, isn't that enough?

WOMAN   What about licking the dirt off them? But not now. Stay there until I have given your daughter the honour of sleeping with the King.

GIRL   What do you want from me?

WOMAN   Cherries dipped in honey.

GIRL   No! *(running away)* Help me! Father! Help me!

MILLER *(covering his ears)* No, no, it's a test.

The WOMAN approaches the GIRL, laughing.

(covering his eyes) I won't get angry. No, I won't.

The WOMAN is raping the GIRL behind the millstone.

GIRL Oh, Father, help me! His knife is on my throat! Help!

CHIEF COMMANDER This is unheard of – a fairy tale. The King unfolding himself to the baseness of such a harlot! He, who had three thousand lovers in his harem, each one more ravishing than the last.

GIRL *(coming out from behind the millstone)* If there was some flour left, I'd make myself white from head to toe.

MILLER My daughter wasn't always like this. Buried inside, her eyes so dead.

GIRL You are so tall… those shoulders… twice mine. Your strength devours my rejection. I see the devil, through a crack in the wall, galloping away on a grey horse.

MILLER He wanted to test my loyalty. How could I raise my hand against the King? It's an eternal sin! I didn't do it. But now I feel a fire inside me worse than hell itself. There's a mutiny in my heart – a millstone in my chest. I will kill him!

GIRL *(dancing)* I pity this dead man.

WOMAN *(to the GIRL)* Shut up! *(to the MILLER)* Kill him!

MILLER *(stabbing)* I'll kill him! Once! Twice! Three times! Four times! Hit him! Strike! Dead. *(stopping, breathless)* Yes. And I am happy.

CHIEF COMMANDER Is this not enough to prove his guilt to the world?

MAGU The truth will always come forth to speak!

CHIEF COMMANDER *(pulling out his sword)* This is our sentence!

WOMAN But you didn't kill him.

MILLER No, I didn't.

MAGU What a preposterous lie.

MILLER I didn't kill him. None of that was true.

MAGU Then why did you lie?

MILLER After what the King did to my daughter, you'd think me a coward if I didn't take revenge. No, I didn't kill him until he started to toy with me.

CORPORAL Toy with you?

MAGU How?

WOMAN   I have called myself a king and fooled you all. Now I have a mill, a bed and a concubine. Ha! How well you believed my little performance. So I see any vagrant can walk through this door, announce that he is the King and descend to your daughter's bed. Ha! How easy… how easy…

MILLER   Not so easy, no! Where's my club?

WOMAN   She had a beautiful body. Such hospitality.

MILLER   Where is my club? Give it to me.

MAGU   Do you hear this? In this court, he is yelling, asking for his club.

CHIEF COMMANDER   To kill the King.

WOMAN   Who said that I am King? Do you see a divine light in my face? Where is my army? My palace? Slave girls? Do I have a nation?

GIRL   (*weeping*) He has a treasure.

WOMAN   Stolen.

GIRL   Who did he steal it from?

WOMAN   From you. Add up all your wages for all the days of your life. Wouldn't that be a treasure?

MILLER   All the days of my life. I've forgotten when they began.

WOMAN   I've stolen all of them.

MILLER   Then you must be the King. All the days of my life – I've always hoped that one day I'd bring my cry for justice to the King. Now he's here, to whom should I cry to about his injustice? Give me back what you have taken from me, King. The days of my life, my lost hopes and the innocence of my child. (*He starts beating the corpse. The King's men cover their eyes.*)

GIRL   Blood! Blood!

WOMAN   His face sprayed blood.

GIRL   Blood! Blood!

WOMAN   (*sitting beside the corpse*) Tell me, King, how did you find my daughter? Was she well broken? Answer me, great King. Was she an obedient mount?

MILLER   (*hitting the corpse*) I killed him.

WOMAN   Was she obedient when you drove her with your spurs?

MILLER   My club.

WOMAN   Strike.

MILLER   All the days of my life.

WOMAN   Strike.

MILLER   All my wages.

WOMAN   Strike.

GIRL   Strike.

MILLER   I killed him.

GIRL   I pity this dead man. I pity this man. *(sitting beside the corpse, weeping)* Oh, Father, why did they kill you?

WOMAN   Stop saying this craziness.

GIRL   Oh Father, what have they done to you?

WOMAN   Shush! Hold your tongue!

GIRL   Oh my father, why did they kill you?

CORPORAL   Did you hear that?

GIRL   This is my father – sleeping here – a poor miller who never saw a drop of kindness in life, not a drop, not even after he died.

CHIEF COMMANDER   What are you saying? Isn't this the King's bloody face?

WOMAN   You know that the girl has lost her wits.

GIRL   Speak, Father. Answer them. *(speaking as the corpse)* My child, oh my daughter… why did I leave you alone?

MAGU   It is the voice of the dead! No such thing is written in all the holy verses. The truth from the Other world is calling us.

CHIEF COMMANDER   *(confused)* I don't know what to say. *(to the CORPORAL and the MAGU)* Come over here. *(to the family)* This is a war-time consultation. *(gathering the others to him)* Quickly. The girl has just said that this is not the King's body. Has anyone here been near enough to the King to see his face?

CORPORAL   Who had authority to gaze upon the King's beautiful face? He wouldn't show it to just anybody.

CHIEF COMMANDER   But you first recognized that body as the King's.

CORPORAL   It was his crown I recognized. That's how I knew. I've never seen him without his golden mask.

CHIEF COMMANDER   Speak, Magu, you've seen him many times.

MAGU   Yes I've seen him, but never with blood caked on his forehead, his cheeks grey, his mouth gaping and his eyes staring at the ceiling. His whole face is distorted.

CHIEF COMMANDER   We must know. I've never seen him except from behind the royal drapes, or when he was in his battle helmet.

CORPORAL   Now what are we going to do? In this state even his harem couldn't recognize him, let alone his servants, who all lower their eyes in his presence.

CHIEF COMMANDER   If he's the Miller then where is the King?

WOMAN   I've told you already. He ran away, disguised. He wanted to escape, so he fled. What else can I tell you?

MAGU   Woe upon us. *(kicking the corpse)* I gave royal blessing to a worthless Miller.

WOMAN   Look at this. The invaders have conquered the entire land and our soldiers are still taking it out on the peasants.

> *The PRIVATE enters.*

PRIVATE   I found a mortar. Has anyone seen the pestle?

GIRL   Eyes front, soldier! What do you need the pestle for?

PRIVATE   For grinding the Miller's bones.

CHIEF COMMANDER   If that's the Miller's body, then who is this man?

PRIVATE   The prisoner is dying. He's pretty quiet. He mumbles something every now and then, though.

CHIEF COMMANDER   *(to the MILLER)* Who are you, man?

WOMAN   Could we have a few words together in private, just the three of us? It's a family-time consultation.

CHIEF COMMANDER   If it results in what we want to hear, then go ahead – but if not... alas. *(to the PRIVATE)* Stay outside and watch the door. *(to the CORPORAL)* Barricade the exits. *(to the MAGU)* Come on. *(to the WOMAN)* And when we come back the face of that man must be cleaned of flour or whatever it is that's covering it. *(to the CORPORAL)* Let's go see the prisoner.

> *The King's men exit, except for the PRIVATE.*

PRIVATE   What kind of chatter is this that we're not allowed to hear?

WOMAN   Just get the hell out.

> *The PRIVATE exits.*

MILLER   What's going on in that head of yours?

WOMAN   You idiot, there's no escaping this. If they think for a moment that this is the King's corpse, our blood will flow, all of us. We must swear over and over that this is not the King.

GIRL   Someone thinks this isn't the Miller's corpse?

MILLER   If that's the Miller then who am I?

WOMAN   Very soon they'll be asking you that same question.

MILLER   If I'm not the Miller, then I'm the King. That's right, right?

WOMAN   You have no choice. If you are not the King then you are the killer of the King and all of us will die. Which do you prefer, to be a king or to be dead?

MILLER   Hmmmm… I see your point.

GIRL   *(crying)* You were never good to my father! You wouldn't even sleep with him. He, who has always wept for his poverty, wept for want of your softness. I hate you!

WOMAN   What would you have me do? I've spent every day of my life with him, in this dungeon with him, like two mules dragging the millstone around. Don't make me regret your birth even more. I admit it was me who brought you to this world and I never expected your gratitude for that.

MILLER   Stop this! *(to the GIRL)* And you, don't speak like—

GIRL   Don't talk to me. Don't touch me, stranger. You, who have seduced her.

MILLER   It's me, me, you fool. Don't you recognize me?

GIRL   Oh yes, I know you very well. I know what kind of man you are. Were there a buyer for me you would barter me for one smile from this woman.

WOMAN   What can I do, girl? Those who would sell you want to buy me.

MILLER   Will you stop this? While we fight in here, out there our graves are being dug. Enough.

GIRL   *(lying on the corpse)* Why Father? Father, Father, why didn't you take me away with you?

MILLER   She truly believes he is the Miller.

WOMAN   It's not such a bad thing. Her insanity will help us, not her reason. Oh my poor girl. She doesn't even know who she is.

The King's men re-renter.

CHIEF COMMANDER   *(to the PRIVATE)* Did you hear anything?

PRIVATE   No, sir. I just peeped through the hole.

CHIEF COMMANDER   Our prisoner told us a few things before he died. We must gather our troops immediately. The enemy is retreating.

PRIVATE   Retreating? This is good news!

CHIEF COMMANDER   Yes it would be, were the King still alive. *(to the WOMAN)* Well, has your little meeting been fruitful?

WOMAN   As a matter of fact we were just watering the tree.

CHIEF COMMANDER   Don't let your toil rot on the branches – harvest.

WOMAN   It's not an easy thing to do. Priest, I will be forced to break an oath. Is it allowed?

MAGU   There is one path and that is the path of truth. All the others are astray.

WOMAN   The girl is right. It is the Miller who is lying there.

CHIEF COMMANDER   What did you say?

MAGU   Strengthen that with a mortal vow.

WOMAN   I swear on the good name of the church.

MAGU   If this is the Miller… (*kicking the corpse*) then who is he?

WOMAN   (*dressing the MILLER*) The King.

CHIEF COMMANDER   Did you hear that?

CORPORAL   Unbelievable…

WOMAN   Yet true. Knights, commanders. Our Miller died a natural death and the man you see standing alive before you is the King. He chose to hide from his people and so disguised himself in the Miller's clothes.

CHIEF COMMANDER   It's a dream come true.

MAGU   Why didn't you say this from the start?

WOMAN   I was bound by oath to keep the secret.

CHIEF COMMANDER   Then he was testing us. I hope I didn't say anything I shouldn't have.

CORPORAL   (*kneeling*) O King.

CHIEF COMMANDER   What is the King's command?

MILLER   Get away from me. Leave me here in my loneliness and never tell a soul you have seen me.

CORPORAL   Anything else, O King.

WOMAN   He abdicates.

MILLER   Should I have told you I was coming here? Then soon the whole world would know. Better to disappear without a trace, without leaving a shadow. Better to be thought dead.

MAGU   These are wise words.

CHIEF COMMANDER   How you must have suffered. We can only bow before you.

CORPORAL   If you really are the true King, O Majesty, then what is my name?

WOMAN   Why should a king trifle to remember the name of a lackey?

CORPORAL   It's a kingly response, but we must be sure. Isn't there anyone in the legion who has seen the King's face?

CHIEF COMMANDER   Will you dare test the King?

CORPORAL   Yes. Now that his face is clean someone might be able to recognize him.

PRIVATE   If you promise not to kill me I'll confess to an unspeakable sin. I once stole a look at the King's heavenly face. It was in the Hunting Enclave. I heard the cry of a falcon. Then I saw him… but only for the blink of an eye… and it was from far away… to tell you the truth, I'm not actually sure whether it was his real face or a fake. You know how he hated to be recognized. Every morning he would have his hair and his make-up changed. Now I think about it, there's absolutely no way to recognize him.

MAGU   *(coming forward)* The King used to have the fragrance of rosewater surrounding him, but all I can smell in this place is the stench of mouldy straw. But I know a way.

> *The MAGU and the King's men put the robe and crown on the MILLER.*

WOMAN   *(to the MILLER)* Take them.

PRIVATE   It isn't him, I swear. In the crown and cloak he's even more royal than our King ever was.

CHIEF COMMANDER   Another test.

MAGU   Walk. Laugh. Turn around. Close your eyes. Now bulge them out. Yell. Roar. Whisper. Raise your arms. Hands on waist. Cross your arms. *(helplessly)* I can't tell either way.

CORPORAL   Look at these callouses, these wrinkles. These are labourer's hands, not the hands of a king.

MILLER   *(clapping his hands)* Are they not?

CHIEF COMMANDER   If you are the King, tell me how many chambers there are in the Palace of the Kings.

WOMAN   The Black Chambers for the Traitors, the Ruby Chambers for the Harem, the Crystal Chamber for the Players. Any other questions?

CHIEF COMMANDER   That's right! That's right! Tell us something else.

WOMAN   The Imperial Carpet is embroidered with eleven hundred and eleven flawless diamonds.

CHIEF COMMANDER   That's right! That's right!

MAGU   I'm the only one who knows the precise number of concubines in the King's harem. What is it?

WOMAN   Two hundred two and twenty.

MAGU   The very number.

MILLER   *(to the WOMAN)* How the hell do you know all this?

WOMAN   You told me. Don't you remember, O King?

MILLER   No, I didn't.

WOMAN   Yes, you told me the number of chambers, diamonds and lovers. Who else could have told me?

MILLER   He did! When he sent me out in the rain. He told you – the King.

WOMAN   You are the King.

MILLER   No, he's not me! I am me – the Miller – a poor and unfortunate man, with hands soaked in blood. Speak up. Did he tell you all this?

WOMAN   Yes, he did.

GIRL   Yes, he.

CHIEF COMMANDER   Separate them. What's going on? What's the story here?

GIRL   Story? *(walking)* I saw it with my own eyes. *(smiling)* Me, the one they thought was worthless.

MILLER   Tell us.

GIRL   He wanted to seduce my mother.

WOMAN   It's a lie.

GIRL   Your wife.

CHIEF COMMANDER   Don't insult the King.

MILLER   I have no trust for this woman. This isn't the first time she's run off to another man.

WOMAN   You spineless—

MILLER   I know everything, all of it.

WOMAN   Everybody has a secret admirer once in a while.

MILLER   All the neighbours?

WOMAN   If I didn't go to them, who would buy our bread?

GIRL   When haven't you betrayed my father?

WOMAN   Was it "betrayal" the year of the famine, when I saved you from dying?

MAGU   How could one think to find the Pure One in a room filled with such filthy words? The age of red moons and black suns has come. We must send out a warning from coast to coast, a message of spiritual guidance.

WOMAN   Send your letter, priest, but be sure to slip in something to eat. We people are already stuffed full of advice, but we still have room for bread. Don't look at me like that. *(to the MILLER)* Yes it's true, I've been waiting years to find a way out of here. Yes, I.

GIRL   *(walking)* He wanted to seduce my mother. He whispered in the dark. The flame of the fire was between them.

MILLER   Where was I?

GIRL   Out in the rain.

MILLER   It was early in the night, wasn't it?

GIRL   Yes, yes it was. Right after the King made a dog of the Miller.

MILLER   *(falling on all fours)* Ruff! Ruff! Ruff!

GIRL   Louder. Louder. Give me the crown, the cloak. Now tell me one more time – who am I?

MILLER   You are the King, my lord.

GIRL   And you, you son of a tramp, who are you?

MILLER   I am the King's dog – the Miller.

GIRL   You miserable curse. Tell me – everything you have, you got from whom?

MILLER   Everything we have we got from the King.

WOMAN   What are you talking about? We've got nothing.

MILLER   That, too, is from the King.

GIRL   The girl – she was for the King's taking. Ahhh! This cold is chilling my soul! Make me a fire. It's pouring outside. The sky looks like an angry sea. Fetch me something to eat – a lamb.

MILLER   A lamb? There is a famine in the land. Many have died already.

GIRL   Go to the nearest village. Search in every alley. When you find someone with a lamb, tell them it belongs to the King. Use force. Steal it if you must – you should know how to do that.

MILLER   It's freezing out there. You can't send me out into the storm.

GIRL   Take a torch with you and do not return without food.

MILLER   The village is far off. Two hours at least.

GIRL   If you find cooked meat, so much the better. If not, a fresh lamb will do.

MILLER It's pitch black. I'll lose my way in the storm.

GIRL What did you say to a king's order?

MILLER *(consenting)* Your will is my command.

GIRL Wait. Even a lizard wouldn't venture out on a night like this. What are you up to? Yes... I have my suspicions about you... you are planning to betray me, aren't you, to reveal my hiding place?

MILLER I wasn't thinking that.

GIRL You know my hideaway. There are those who would pay handsomely for this information.

MILLER You're putting these thoughts into my head, my King.

GIRL Remember, I have your wife and daughter here – and a sword in my hand. Whenever the thought runs through your head, remember this.

WOMAN Even bandits haven't done such things to us.

GIRL Are you comparing me, the King, to a bandit?

WOMAN I've seen bandits be generous to the poor, but never a king.

MILLER I will go. Oh, will I never be free of this woman?

WOMAN Free of me? You love me. Wherever you go you will come back to me. Haven't you tried to leave many times before?

MILLER I left, bending under a black rain that hid the fields from my sight. The world around was like a wild sea, and in it the mill was sinking. I travelled far off in search of food and wood, but all the time my thoughts remained behind, in the mill, with the King.

GIRL *(as the King to herself)* Why should I die? Why should I freeze in the hands of death? My enemies have lost me in the storm. I've chopped off my hair, shaved my beard – perhaps I won't be recognized. It is possible... yes... it is possible I could live for years in happiness. If only they believed I was dead, they would give up their pursuit.

WOMAN What's he thinking?

GIRL It is possible. Only the woman and that girl know my whole story. But the girl is an imbecile, so all that remains is the woman.

WOMAN He was there with me. The King and I, alone. I the Miller's wife, trapped in a monotony of coarseness and coarse people all my life. He's gazing at me through the fire. What's he thinking?

GIRL Yes, it is possible.

WOMAN I'm terrified. My heart feels like a dove.

GIRL   She has a beautiful body, the Miller's wife. She's been through such hardship, such pain and hunger – she will surrender to me.

WOMAN   What do you want from me?

GIRL   Woman, how do you feel about your husband?

WOMAN   I feel he loves me.

GIRL   And you?

WOMAN   Me? Do you see any reason to doubt it? I pity him. He should never have left. What am I doing? What will become of him?

GIRL   Why are you trembling?

WOMAN   He has suffered through so much. So have I. So have I.

GIRL   I desire you.

WOMAN   No!

GIRL   Come over here.

WOMAN   You're frightening me.

MILLER   Go to hell, woman!

WOMAN   Why? Have I had a moment of joy with you? I was a young woman when I set foot into this darkness, and ever since I've had two stones for companions – that one, and you.

GIRL   Oh Father! Oh Father! Why did they kill you?

CORPORAL   No, child. You were telling the King's story.

GIRL   I hate you, Mother, I hate you! *(The WOMAN slaps her face. The GIRL smiles.)* Yes, what a fine slap you gave the King when he told you his secret.

WOMAN   Don't. No more. You love me – don't say it.

GIRL   The Miller is a nothing. Are you not weary of him? Do you not dream to have a taste of happiness? Be with me.

WOMAN   That's what he said. My heart pounded. Tell me more, my King.

GIRL   You're so firm. I'm falling in love with you. In a storm like this, what could be warmer than your body.

WOMAN   *(weeping)* Could it be true? Somebody help me. Someone show me the way.

GIRL   You will be freed…

WOMAN   From the whirlpool.

GIRL   And I shall hold you.

WOMAN   Like you held my daughter?

GIRL   That wasn't love, not at all – that was provocation. I wanted you to hate me, you and the Miller. I wanted you to kill me.

WOMAN   You won't die.

GIRL   What did you say?

WOMAN   How can I be free of my husband?

GIRL   I'm looking for a dead body – a poor man wearing a king's costumes. Have you seen any such person?

WOMAN   It's a frightening thought.

GIRL   They will all believe he is the King. What more splendid an end than this for your husband?

WOMAN   No one is without sin.

GIRL   Together on the saddle of my horse, my treasures will last us 'til the end of time.

WOMAN   Will I be freed then?

GIRL   Well? Have you decided?

WOMAN   You are younger.

GIRL   And more graceful. I rose from Solomon's throne, walked the Imperial Carpet, eleven hundred and eleven perfect diamonds cool against my feet. I went to my lovers – two hundred two and twenty strong.

WOMAN   In the Palace of the Kings?

GIRL   Thirty-three corridors led to my throne with seven chambers on all sides. The Black Chambers for Traitors, the Ruby Chambers for the Harem and the Crystal Chamber for the Players.

WOMAN   Ahhh, girl! So you heard all this?

GIRL   And more. Oh, let me slip between your thighs…

WOMAN   Don't!

GIRL   You're so firm. I'm falling in love with you. In a storm like this, what could be warmer than your body.

WOMAN   You heard it all.

GIRL   The Miller is nothing. Close your eyes, kill him, stuff him in my robes and flee. Everyone will believe his corpse is mine.

WOMAN   The girl, what about the girl?

GIRL That silly slave-girl? Even if she survives, the enemy's horses will trample her.

WOMAN Then kill her…

GIRL It is the better fate.

WOMAN Kill…

GIRL *(yelling)* Now my father is coming! *(The MILLER advances furiously.)* Back from the heart of darkness, back from the eye of the storm!

WOMAN Kill!

MILLER *(attacking the corpse)* Beast! *(The WOMAN screams, collapsing in the GIRL's arms.)* Yes, he attacked me. Your King. *(sitting beside the corpse)* The warrior and his sword. He descended upon me like Death herself, and I killed him.

CORPORAL Then he killed himself?

WOMAN *(yelling)* Where is salvation?

> The PRIVATE enters.

PRIVATE The gallows are up, the graves are dug, the mortar and pestle are waiting and the oven is red hot.

MILLER My wife, my daughter. You are victims of my poverty. I'm leaving this twin, this helplessness. They say the invaders are coming. If I had some dates and bread I would welcome them home.

CHIEF COMMANDER Dismantle the gallows, cool down the oven. I've changed my verdict.

MAGU And mine.

CORPORAL Mine, too.

CHIEF COMMANDER But our story will stay the same. Hang this dead body.

PRIVATE The King?

CHIEF COMMANDER Immediately. He is the Miller. *(to the CORPORAL)* Tell me when it's done. *(to the MAGU)* Don't you have some praying to do?

CORPORAL Come on. The victorious write history.

> The CORPORAL and the PRIVATE take the corpse out. The MAGU exits with them.

CHIEF COMMANDER What are you looking at? I'm throwing this uniform away. This is a hopeless war. He created a universe we couldn't defend. What are you staring at?

WOMAN   Look, Miller, from where you saw the ragged King descending, now look at the invaders, coming after him.

CORPORAL   *(running in)* The judgement hasn't ended yet. We've been hunted by death all this time without knowing it. There's a sea of troops out there. They don't greet us good day or good night. They do not reason, nor will they listen to any. They speak with their swords.

MAGU   *(running in)* We're trapped! The invaders! The invaders!

PRIVATE   *(running in)* Draw your swords! Get the lances! Drums!

CHIEF COMMANDER   It's pointless. Pray to death. She's standing at the threshold, immense as a desert. And when raised by the storm, she lowers the eyes of the world.

WOMAN   Yes, now the real judges are here. You and your white flag gave us this sentence. Let's wait for the verdict of this black one.

    Blackout.

Stories from the Rains of Love and Death

Abas Na'lbandian

Translated by Soheil Parsa with Peter Farbridge

Andrew Scorer, Peter Farbridge
photo by Karen Braaten

Stories from the Rains of Love and Death was first produced by Modern Times Stage Company at Artword Mainspace, Toronto from November 3 to 23, 2003, with the following company:

MAN/TEACHER	Stewart Arnott
DAUGHTER	Nita Costa
SON	Mark Ellis
METZ/MO	Peter Farbridge
FATHER	John Gilbert
BOY	Daniel Karasik
MOTHER/MOTHER	Stavroula Logothettis
HADZ/HAMON	Andrew Scorer

Director: Soheil Parsa
Set Designer: David Skelton
Lighting Designer: Andrea Lundy
Costume Designer: Angela Thomas
Sound Designer: Thomas Payne
Producer: Laurel Smith

• • •

Awards and Nominations
Dora Mavor Moore Awards: Outstanding Direction (Soheil Parsa), Outstanding Lighting Design (Andrea Lundy), and Outstanding New Play or Musical (Abas Na'lbandian, translation by Soheil Parsa and Peter Farbridge). Dora Mavor Moore Nominations: Outstanding Costume Design (Angela Thomas), Outstanding Set Design (David Skelton).

Characters

THE FIRST FOLD
DAUGHTER
MOTHER
MAN

THE SECOND FOLD
HADZ
METZ

THE THIRD FOLD
SON
FATHER
MOTHER

THE FOURTH FOLD
TEACHER
BOY

THE FIFTH FOLD
MO
HAMON

Stories from the Rains of Love and Death

THE FIRST FOLD

<u>Black Rains, Death</u>

A room with the simple furniture of a lower class family: a huge old radio; a wooden dresser; an old rug. A lightbulb hangs from the ceiling. On the right of the room is a door, and to the left there is a mattress with a blanket and two pillows. There is a bulge in the blanket, as if a body were underneath. The MOTHER and DAUGHTER are standing over the bed. The DAUGHTER is frightened.

DAUGHTER   Is he dead?

MOTHER   Yes.

DAUGHTER   No.

MOTHER   *(sarcastically)* Yeah!

DAUGHTER   Oh, God!

MOTHER   Don't look!

DAUGHTER   No!

MOTHER   Keep it down!

DAUGHTER   *(moving away from the MOTHER)* I'm scared.

MOTHER   Calm down!

DAUGHTER   His eyes are open.

MOTHER   Stay back!

DAUGHTER   He's not dead! His eyes…

MOTHER   Shut up!

DAUGHTER   *(running away)* Help!

MOTHER   *(chasing her)* Shut up!

DAUGHTER   *(crashing into the wall)* Oh! What happened?

MOTHER   You're freaking me out!

DAUGHTER   He's not moving, Ma!

MOTHER   He's dead!

DAUGHTER   His face!

MOTHER   You're scaring me!

DAUGHTER   We've got to call the neighbours.

MOTHER   And humiliate ourselves?

DAUGHTER   Why?

MOTHER   You think they won't wanna know what the hell he was doing in our bed?

DAUGHTER   Huh?

MOTHER   What if they think we killed him?

DAUGHTER   In our bed?

MOTHER   In your bed.

DAUGHTER   Yeah.

MOTHER   What happened?

DAUGHTER   He was lying down beside me.

MOTHER   Then? *(The DAUGHTER is choked with tears.)* Then? *(The DAUGHTER starts to weep.)* Had he finished? *(The DAUGHTER is weeping.)* He's butt-naked then. We'll have to get his pants back on.

DAUGHTER   Maybe he's still alive.

MOTHER   No.

DAUGHTER   Maybe he's just passed out.

MOTHER   Then what happened?

DAUGHTER   He was on top of me... and... all of a sudden he stopped moving.

MOTHER   We gotta be careful with this.

DAUGHTER   I didn't know at first.

MOTHER   What did you do?

DAUGHTER   I was scared.

MOTHER   So you screamed.

DAUGHTER   I was scared and I screamed so you'd come. I pushed him off and jumped out of bed.

MOTHER   Something's screwed up here.

DAUGHTER   We should call the cops.

MOTHER   I hear someone.

DAUGHTER   Maybe the neighbours woke up.

MOTHER   Get his pants on!

DAUGHTER   Let's get out of here, Ma!

> *The DAUGHTER goes under the blanket beside the MAN. The MOTHER sits on the floor, facing the audience.*

You're hurting me!

MAN   Relax!

DAUGHTER   Don't squeeze me there!

MAN   Shut up!

DAUGHTER   You're so heavy!

MAN   Oh yes.

DAUGHTER   Why'd you say it was me who hit you on the head?

MAN   I never said such a thing-a-ding?

DAUGHTER   Liar. *(pause)* Why'd you lie?

MAN   Wait! Wait!

DAUGHTER   You know it wasn't me. *(pause)* When will I ever get rid of you?

MAN   You won't.

DAUGHTER   Your face makes me sick.

MAN   Whatever.

DAUGHTER   Move your hand.

MAN   Oh, d'ya have to piss on my party every time?

DAUGHTER   I wish I could yank this thing from between your legs and smash it in your fuckin' face.

MAN   Watch your mouth.

DAUGHTER   Come on, finish up. I'm suffocating. *(pause)* What's wrong with you?

> *She screams, throws off the MAN to the side, runs and takes refuge against the wall. The MOTHER gets up, goes to the radio and turns it on.*

FIRST WOMAN   *(voice-over)* Grab the other leg! Pull him!

SECOND WOMAN   *(voice-over)* What if he gets stuck halfway?

FIRST WOMAN   *(voice-over)* It's a big well; he'll make it down.

SECOND WOMAN   *(voice-over)* What if they find out?

FIRST WOMAN   *(voice-over)* We got him all the way here, didn't we, and did anybody notice?

SECOND WOMAN   *(voice-over)* Someone could come.

FIRST WOMAN   *(voice-over)* Pull! Harder! Throw him in!

>   *The sound of a heavy object falling. The MOTHER turns off the radio.*

DAUGHTER   Say something!

MOTHER   Be quiet, I'm thinking.

DAUGHTER   We gotta call the cops.

MOTHER   Right, that's all we need.

DAUGHTER   It can't get any worse than this.

MOTHER   What?

DAUGHTER   It looks like we killed him whatever we do.

MOTHER   What if they don't find out?

DAUGHTER   What?

MOTHER   What if they don't find out?

DAUGHTER   They will.

MOTHER   What if he was never here?

DAUGHTER   What?

MOTHER   What if he was never here?

DAUGHTER   Are you saying we should get rid of him?

MOTHER   Why not?

DAUGHTER   Where to?

MOTHER   Wherever.

DAUGHTER   Can't be done.

MOTHER   Why not?

DAUGHTER   We'll be caught.

MOTHER   No.

DAUGHTER   We'll be caught and put away.

MOTHER   We'll throw him in a ditch.

DAUGHTER   He's heavy. He's too heavy.

MOTHER   Well, both of us will…

DAUGHTER   I'm scared. I won't touch him.

MOTHER   Shut up.

DAUGHTER   I won't touch a dead man. I won't.

MOTHER   Pee-ewe!

DAUGHTER   I'm gonna barf.

MOTHER   Hold it back.

DAUGHTER   I can't.

> *The MOTHER goes under the blanket beside the MAN. The DAUGHTER sits on the floor, facing the audience.*

MOTHER   Go to hell!

MAN   Relax!

MOTHER   Drop dead!

MAN   Shut up.

MOTHER   Are you done?

MAN   Getting there.

MOTHER   That was a shitty move to ask for your money in front of everyone.

MAN   I never said such a thing-a-ding?

MOTHER   Oh fuck-a-duck! Get off me you goddamn jerk!

MAN   Wait! Wait!

MOTHER   You're so used to this, eh? Calling in every night now?

MAN   We already talked about that.

MOTHER   Your money's gonna be late this month.

MAN   Whatever.

MOTHER   And tell the landlord to give us a break.

MAN   For fuck's sake, do you have to piss on my party every time?

MOTHER   I wish I could yank this thing from between your legs and smash it in your fucking face.

MAN   Watch your mouth!

MOTHER   Come on, finish up. I'm suffocating. *(pause)* What's wrong with you?

> *The MOTHER screams, throws off the MAN to the side, runs and takes refuge against the wall. The DAUGHTER gets up, goes to the radio and turns it on.*

FIRST MAN   *(voice-over)* Shake off your coat; it's dusty.

SECOND MAN   *(voice-over)* I feel much better now.

FIRST MAN   *(voice-over)* Remember, we haven't seen each other at all today.

SECOND MAN   *(voice-over)* Right. There better not be any hassle.

FIRST MAN   *(voice-over)* There won't be. Just act normal.

SECOND MAN   *(voice-over)* I feel much better now.

> *Loud laughter. The DAUGHTER turns off the radio.*

MOTHER   Let's put his pants back on.

DAUGHTER   Do it yourself.

MOTHER   Quit acting like a baby already. We got a long way to go together.

DAUGHTER   Let's call the cops.

MOTHER   Close that door!

DAUGHTER   What door?

MOTHER   What was that noise then?

DAUGHTER   We'll tell the truth.

MOTHER   What truth?

DAUGHTER   That he came here.

MOTHER   They'll arrest us.

DAUGHTER   Huh?

MOTHER   Yes.

DAUGHTER   At least let's wait.

MOTHER   For what? *(pause)* I'm hungry.

DAUGHTER   'Til it gets darker.

MOTHER   Darker than this?

DAUGHTER   He's heavy.

MOTHER   Not really.

DAUGHTER   Yes.

MOTHER   What?

DAUGHTER   Why?

MOTHER   I'm hungry. Let's eat first.

DAUGHTER   I don't feel good. I can hardly breathe.

MOTHER   Set the table.

During the following conversation they set the table and bring in the food.

DAUGHTER   How we gonna take him?

MOTHER   Take him where?

DAUGHTER   To wherever it is we're going.

MOTHER   We'll chuck him in a ditch. *(pause)* In a well.

DAUGHTER   How we gonna take him?

MOTHER   Put him in a sack.

DAUGHTER   What sack?

MOTHER   That big one.

DAUGHTER   That's not ours.

MOTHER   Is the corpse ours?

DAUGHTER   How do we sneak him down the hall?

MOTHER   On our backs.

DAUGHTER   What about the door?

MOTHER   What are you talking about?

DAUGHTER   Poor guy didn't even have his dinner.

MOTHER   How do you know that?

DAUGHTER   Maybe.

> *The table is set. They sit and eat very slowly. The lights dim until the characters can hardly be seen. The MAN gets up and very gently creeps to the table. Lights slowly fade to black.*

THE SECOND FOLD

Night Rains, Cold

> *A room with one door, stage left. A bed is opposite the door. In the room, a propane tank, a small propane stove, a lightbulb is hanging from the ceiling. The room's a mess. It's nighttime and the lights are on. HADZ[1] is lying down on the bed. The door opens and METZ enters. He is carrying a bag and some bread.*

HADZ   You're here?

METZ   Who are you?

---

[1] In Abas Na'lbandian's script, Metz and Hadz were called Mohammed and Hamid.

HADZ   Shhh!

METZ   *(screaming)* Thief!

HADZ   Be careful, you'll drop it.

METZ   What? *(pause)* Thief!

> *HADZ blows through his lips.*

What are you doing?

HADZ   Blow!

METZ   Get out of here!

HADZ   What'd you get for dinner?

METZ   Get out! *(pause)* Dinner?

HADZ   Scrambled eggs again?

METZ   What's it to you?

HADZ   I've been waiting here for ages.

METZ   Waiting for what?

HADZ   You.

METZ   Me?

HADZ   Why don't you come in?

METZ   Thief!

HADZ   Your arm's going to get tired.

METZ   No, it won't.

HADZ   You're tired.

METZ   I'm not.

HADZ   Why you being so stubborn?

METZ   You want me to call the police?

HADZ   Ha?

METZ   The police.

HADZ   Didn't you have scrambled last night?

METZ   So?

HADZ   And for lunch again today?

METZ   Yeah, so?

HADZ   You should have got something different.

METZ   Like?

HADZ   Like a sandwich or something.

> *HADZ gets off the bed. The bag and bread fall from METZ's hand.*

Why did you fight with him today?

METZ   With whom?

> *Silence.*

With whom?

> *HADZ is staring at METZ.*

It just happened. *(pause)* He was getting on my nerves again.

HADZ   You're lying.

METZ   No.

HADZ   Yes.

METZ   No, I'm not.

HADZ   You broke the eggs. *(pause)* Aren't you going to clean them up? Why don't you hook up the new tank to the stove?

METZ   Get out! Get out of here! Get out of my room!

HADZ   He was really pissed at you.

METZ   Fuck him.

> *Lights go to black.*

HADZ   Shake off your coat! It's dusty!

METZ   I feel better now.

HADZ   Remember, we never saw each other today.

METZ   Right. There better not be any hassle.

HADZ   There won't be. Just act normal.

METZ   I feel better now.

> *Lights fade up.*

HADZ   Are you going to stand there all night?

METZ   What?

HADZ   Aren't you going to eat?

METZ   I'm dizzy. I gotta sleep.

HADZ   Then eat your dinner and hit the hay.

METZ   Yeah.

HADZ   He was really pissed at you.

METZ   I didn't do anything to him.

HADZ   Why did you hit him on the head?

METZ   When?

> *METZ sits down where he is. HADZ approaches him.*

HADZ   I need a big sack with no holes.

METZ   I gotta sleep.

HADZ   We should get out of the city.

METZ   It's too dark.

HADZ   We've got to get him in the sack.

METZ   I'm tired.

> *HADZ moves away. METZ picks up the bag and gets up. Lights fade to black.*

He stuffed it all in the sack. I'm tired. I should just eat something and go to bed. How hard does a guy have to work? How much do I have to lick these fuckers' balls. I shoulda bought a sandwich tonight. Scrambled eggs for lunch and the same thing again. I can't change that. I should change the tanks on the stove. I tell him: "Get off my back, I'm not in the mood." Does he listen? I should've hit his fucking head with the crowbar, the motherfucker.

> *Lights up. METZ puts the bag on the bed and searches around.*

HADZ   What are you looking for?

METZ   I can't find the fork.

HADZ   Under the bed!

METZ   No.

HADZ   Yes!

METZ   No.

HADZ   Well, take a look!

METZ   Is this your business?

HADZ   To hell with you then, don't look!

METZ   I don't know where I put it. *(He checks under the bed.)* Ah. Here it is.
      I should've smashed his head with the crowbar! I know he'll blame the whole

thing on me. It was the sack that was rotten. I told him so. I told him from the start. Couldn't see the bottom of the well. He was so heavy. I'm dead tired. Thank God I'm home. I'm lucky it didn't storm. It's like he's following me all the time. I turn around and look behind me. *(He looks around.)*

HADZ   What are you looking for?

METZ   The saltshaker.

HADZ   Under the bed.

METZ   It's strange.

HADZ   But you need to fill it up.

METZ   I know I put it somewhere. *(He nervously searches.)* Fuck! Fuck!

HADZ   It's under the bed.

METZ   *(stopping and turning to HADZ)* Who are you? What do you want here?

HADZ   Shhh!

>   *Lights fade out.*

METZ   I'm forgetting everything. Am I losing my mind? No, it's nothing. Then why am I talking to myself? When? When? Just now I was talking to myself. No, there was someone else. Someone else? Who? There's no one here. Yes, there is. You're freaking me out. I'm scared. What are you scared of? You're saying someone's here. Well what's so scary about that? It's not scary? You walk to a room and find a stranger? *(He laughs loudly and stops abruptly. Lights up.)* Don't laugh! I'm so scared.

HADZ   Shhh!

METZ   What?

HADZ   Blow!

METZ   What are you doing?

HADZ   Blow!

METZ   Who are you?

HADZ   You!

METZ   What?

HADZ   You!

METZ   I'm going crazy. There's someone in the room with me.

HADZ   There's no one here.

METZ   Then why is my heart pounding?

HADZ   Anxiety.

METZ   My head's full. It's bursting—

HADZ   It's nothing—

METZ   Like someone's talking to me.

HADZ   Saying what?

METZ   He's arguing with me.

HADZ   About what?

METZ   He's torturing me.

HADZ   You're exhausted.

METZ   What should I do?

HADZ   Eat your dinner and go to bed.

METZ   *(stops moving for a second)* You're right.

> *During the following conversation, METZ hooks up the tank to the stove, sets the table and prepares scrambled eggs. HADZ watches him.*

HADZ   You've got to sleep.

METZ   Yeah.

HADZ   But first, shake off your coat.

METZ   What for?

HADZ   To get rid of the dust.

METZ   You're right, I completely forgot.

HADZ   If the sack wasn't rotten this wouldn't have happened. His thumb stuck out of a hole.

METZ   My heart almost stopped.

HADZ   I was sweating all over. Shaking like a leaf. I kept telling him: "Help me out!" But he couldn't stop bawling.

METZ   I dropped the sack and hit him on the head.

HADZ   Hit him on the chest, in the gut, on the face, the motherfucker. I was out of breath. I didn't know what else to do. He said someone's laughing at us. I said I wish we had some vodka. Someone's laughing at us.

METZ   A dog was barking.

HADZ   I poured the vodka on the sack.

METZ   I lit a match.

HADZ Set the sack on fire.

METZ Suddenly—

HADZ Fire was everywhere; we ran for it.

METZ Ran for it.

HADZ Someone was laughing. I lost my shoes. Son of a bitch!

METZ And now—

HADZ We should clean up our clothes and get some sleep. Is this pathetic excuse for a meal ever going to be ready?

METZ Yeah.

HADZ Let's eat here.

> *They sit and start eating their eggs, very slowly. From now to the end of the scene, the bulb hanging from the ceiling gradually fades out. Only the tiny light of the stove will illuminate the stage.*

I was terrified when I opened the door.

METZ I thought I saw someone on my bed.

HADZ But it was the sack…

METZ …that was growing.

HADZ The sack that was rotten.

METZ The sack that had holes.

HADZ It was the sack with the thumb sticking out.

METZ The sack that was swollen.

HADZ The sack that was stinking.

METZ & HADZ *(Their voices get gradually louder.)* Pah! I was terrified. I was sweating. The wind was blowing. Blowing the smell. A dog was barking. I couldn't see the bottom of the well. The sack left a dent in the bedsheet. I hit my head with the crowbar. My brain flew from my mouth. My eyes exploded. The stove caught fire. Someone yelled: "Blow! Blow!" The stove went out. I was tired. I'm tired. I have to clean up my clothes. In the hallway. I ran into the wall. Got dusty. *(The door opens quietly.)* Bury him in the dirt. The motherfucker's laughing.

> *They laugh for a moment and stop abruptly. A huge, dusty sack filled with a human body rolls heavily across the floor. The stove bursts into flames and then goes out. Darkness.*

THE THIRD FOLD

Wine Rains, White

A porch surrounded by a short, worn out wooden fence. A single bed with a table and chair beside it. On the table, a large vase of red roses. Branches of white jasmine cover the wall in the back. Another chair, far from the bed, is against the wall. In this chair sits the MOTHER, in a long white dress. She remains there throughout the scene. The SON is lying down on the bed and the FATHER is standing. Moonlight.

MOTHER   Why didn't you tell us there was a corpse nearby?

FATHER   You've become very weak. You should rest up – I told you so.

SON   I'm fine, Father. I get a bit dizzy when I walk, that's all.

MOTHER   Why didn't you tell us there was a corpse nearby?

FATHER   I told you to take care of yourself. You see how a simple illness can get out of hand?

MOTHER   It's too late now.

SON   It's too late now.

FATHER   Are you going to sleep out here tonight?

MOTHER   With the jasmine?

FATHER   What if there's a storm?

MOTHER   Wouldn't it be better to sleep inside?

SON   Could be… I don't know.

   Silence.

So, have you gone to the doctor?

FATHER   Doctor?

SON   Yes, for the chest pain and—

MOTHER   *(brusquely)* There's nothing wrong with him!

FATHER   No, I haven't got the time. Ah, to hell with it. It'll get better by itself.

SON   No, Father, you must go to the doctor.

MOTHER   You're sick. There is a tumour in your lung.

FATHER   I've got no time for these things. Once was more than enough, thank you.

SON   It may get worse.

FATHER   It'll get better by itself. *(pause)* Don't you remember my leg last year? None of the doctors could figure it out. Finally it got better on its own.

SON   This is different.

FATHER   No it's not. You should be thinking of yourself right now. Are you going to be able to go to school tomorrow?

SON   Yes, I think so.

MOTHER   Do you remember? It was spring.

SON   *(internally)* When?

MOTHER   It was spring. There was a road beside a forest. The grass was like a blanket between the trees and everything was sparkling. The leaves were rustling in the breeze.

FATHER   Your mother was worried that you'd fall.

> *A long silence.*

Did anyone come to visit you today?

SON   Yes. Mary.

> *Silence.*

FATHER   I want to tell you something.

MOTHER   *(brusquely)* What was that?

SON   What, Father?

FATHER   Recently Mary's been looking at me strangely.

> *The MOTHER laughs knowingly. Silence.*

SON   Strangely?

FATHER   Uh huh.

SON   What do you mean, strangely?

FATHER   I don't know how to describe it. It's very… very unsettling. As if she wants to tell me something, but she can't. Something like that. Are you two still getting along?

SON   Absolutely… very well.

FATHER   It's strange.

> *The MOTHER laughs knowingly.*

If you want to sleep now, I can leave.

SON   No, I slept a lot this afternoon. It's been months since I've had an afternoon nap.

FATHER   It's been months since I've been up at night. I've gotten used to going to bed so early now. *(pause)* Do you remember the days when we'd take trips out of town?

SON   Yes. Mother had just died.

MOTHER   Yes. Then I died. Your father went for a walk while you and I prepared the food. Then suddenly I saw the eyes of a vulture flashing. Flashed. The whole corpse was bloody. Its chest was torn. The vulture's talons were red with blood. Then I died. Your father was watching. Vomiting. The leaves were rustling in the breeze. Wine spilled on my chest. My hands turned red. My dress turned red. Then I died.

FATHER   I'm cold. Have you got any vodka?

SON   I've just got some wine. It's inside.

> The FATHER leaves. Silence. He returns with a bottle of wine and a glass and puts them on the table. He drinks in silence. The SON watches him.

FATHER   Would you like some?

SON   No. Are you cold?

FATHER   No. *(He drinks.)* Cheers.

SON   Cheers. You're not going to eat anything with that?

FATHER   No. Your mother had just died. *(The MOTHER coughs.)* Everywhere I looked, something reminded me of her. Brought tears to my eyes. Do you remember I told you once that this house is becoming strange to me?

SON   Why do you want to go there again?

FATHER   Why not? *(pause)* I can't recall her face anymore. It's horrible. I can't believe it.

MOTHER   I know. It's horrible.

SON   It's natural, Father, not horrible.

FATHER   What?

SON   Forgetting a face.

FATHER   No, it's not natural. It's inhuman.

SON   No, it happens to all of us.

FATHER   And for this reason it's human, is that it?

SON   Yes.

MOTHER   Yes, it's horrible.

FATHER   I disagree. If a plague comes and kills everyone, is it human? If a flood comes and wipes out an entire village, is this human? Can it be said that anything that's common is human?

SON   Why not? Death is.

MOTHER   Death.

FATHER   *(He smiles and drinks.)* Cheers.

SON   Cheers.

> *Silence.*

FATHER   Death.

MOTHER   Death.

FATHER   One word. Five letters. I can't remember your mother's face anymore. As soon as I start to picture it, a kind of wave comes between us, washes it away. *(He gets up and paces.)* What's happening? Why is life getting colder and colder every day?

SON   *(pouring himself some wine)* Cheers.

MOTHER   I'm cold.

FATHER   I'm tired; I feel gloomy. As if someone's beckoning me.

SON   Is something bothering you?

MOTHER   I'm cold.

FATHER   I'm worried.

SON   About what?

MOTHER   I don't know.

FATHER   I don't know, nothing in particular. I just feel like everything is coming apart. Little by little it's all becoming... foreign. *(pause)* I wish you'd get better... although I'm sure it's just the flu.

SON   Why don't you visit the doctor? Both for your chest and—

FATHER   I told you. I hate doctors.

SON   But your chest needs serious attention.

FATHER   I don't think so.

SON   You need an X-ray.

> *The MOTHER coughs. The FATHER laughs.*

FATHER   Again?

SON   Yes.

FATHER   Why?

SON   I don't know, Father. It's just what I think.

FATHER   What do you think?

SON   I mean the doctor said—

FATHER   Said what?

MOTHER   No.

SON   That your chest has to be X-rayed again.

FATHER   *(sits)* Why didn't he tell me this?

SON   Well, because at the time it wasn't necessary.

>   *Silence.*

FATHER   What do you know that I don't?

SON   *(getting up from the bed)* Nothing, Father.

>   *Silence. The SON pours himself more wine and drinks.*

MOTHER   You said you didn't want to drink.

SON   If you're drinking, I might as well, too.

MOTHER   Why haven't you told me? *(pause)* Say it! *(pause)* No. Then I'll die. *(She coughs.)*

FATHER   You make me laugh when you try to hide something from me. You simply can't.

SON   No, Father, I can't.

FATHER   Say it.

SON   You're sick. There's a tumour in your lung.

FATHER   A tumour? I don't believe it. Why hasn't the doctor told me about it?

>   *The MOTHER laughs knowingly.*

SON   Because he didn't want to upset you.

FATHER   Upset me? With what? Isn't it curable?

SON   No, Father.

>   *The MOTHER laughs knowingly.*

FATHER   No?

SON   I mean, no, it's not like that, Father.

> *The SON pours himself some wine and drinks. Silence. He paces. The*
> *moon disappears for a second. Darkness. The moon reappears.*

FATHER   Do you remember the time the three of us went on a trip?

SON   Which time?

FATHER   It was spring. There was a road beside the forest. The grass was a blanket between the trees and everything was sparkling. The leaves were rustling in the breeze.

SON   Yes. I was standing on the back seat screaming for joy.

FATHER   Your mother was worried that you'd fall.

SON   You were laughing.

FATHER   I was laughing.

SON   Do you remember we gave water to that shepherd?

FATHER   Yes. Taking care of his flock. They were grazing. And do you remember the place where we stopped for lunch? Beside that enormous river? The water roaring by…

> *Moonlight goes.*

SON   Yes, we had a picnic on the grass.

> *Moonlight comes.*

FATHER   You stayed there. I went for a walk by the riverbank.

> *Moonlight goes.*

SON   I didn't come with you.

> *Moonlight comes.*

FATHER   No, you didn't come. You were helping your mother prepare the food. Then suddenly my heart stopped. I saw a vulture eating a man, a corpse.

> *Moonlight goes.*

SON   There were only flowers, Father, as far as we could see.

> *Moonlight comes.*

FATHER   There was a corpse, out of your sight. The vulture picked at its heart, looked up with its big eyes, flew around for a while, and came back again. The whole corpse was bloody. The bird's talons were red with blood. Right then I felt something leave me and no matter how hard I reached, I just couldn't grab it. It was unstoppable.

> *Moonlight goes.*

SON   There was no corpse, Father.

Moonlight comes.

FATHER   Perhaps it was life. Do you remember the man who waved at us from across the road? I heard something shatter in my heart. I held my chest. You were preparing the food. The sun was shining and I felt the breeze on my face. The day was passing by. My legs were shaking. I was about to fall down. I thought that the sun had vanished. *(He picks up his glass of wine and throws it at the MOTHER. Her dress and hands are stained red.)* But… *(Moonlight goes. Silence. Darkness.)*

THE FOURTH FOLD

<u>Earth Rains, Love</u>

A small classroom. Chairs and desks in two rows face the audience. Three long, old windows are stage left and a door is stage right. The walls are dirty and have a dull blue colour. At the top of the scene, the exterior of the classroom beyond the window is bright and the classroom is dark, in a way that the TEACHER and the BOY can barely be seen. By the end of the scene, the lighting condition changes: the outside turns completely dark and the classroom extremely bright, to the point that the TEACHER and the BOY can barely be seen. The source of the lights should not be visible to the audience. Lights fade in. The TEACHER is standing in front of the middle window. The BOY is walking towards the door.

TEACHER   Wait!

BOY   *(turning around)* Yes, sir.

TEACHER   Sit down!

BOY   Yes, sir.

He sits behind a desk in the middle of the room.

TEACHER   I've heard something about you. *(pause)* Something that has made me quite upset. That's why I was so distracted in class today.

BOY   Yes, sir.

TEACHER   I want you to tell me the truth. Listen, my boy, I'm like your father. Perhaps sometimes I can be even closer to you than your father. There are things a boy may not be able to tell his parents, but he can tell them to his teacher. Right?

BOY   Yes, sir.

TEACHER   Do you understand what I'm saying?

BOY   No, sir.

TEACHER   Well, then let me simplify it for you. Imagine one day one of the kids in your neighbourhood comes and tells you something. For example... for example, tells you to go to a remote place and undress. Right?

BOY   *(hesitant)* Yes, sir.

TEACHER   Well, of course you won't have the guts to tell this to your parents, but you must be able to tell your teacher. Do you understand what I'm saying now?

BOY   Yes, sir. You mean that if someone says something like that to me I should let you know about it.

TEACHER   Good boy, that's exactly what I meant.

BOY   *(getting up)* All right, sir, I'll let you know for sure.

TEACHER   *(taken aback)* Where are you going? *(The BOY sits immediately.)* Listen, what I've just said was just an example. You must be very careful. All of you must be careful. If anything like this happens to any of you, you should immediately inform your teachers, or there could be terrible consequences.

BOY   Yes, sir.

   Pause.

TEACHER   Now, is there anything that you want to tell me?

   Silence.

BOY   No one has said anything like that to me, sir.

TEACHER   But I've heard something else about you. *(silence)* Ha? *(silence)* You see, my son, I want to help you. Don't be afraid. Tell me about it. *(silence)* I saw you the day before yesterday, coming back to school from lunch. You were with a man. Who was he? *(pause)* Do you remember? The afternoon it was raining? *(A long silence.)*

BOY   *(remembering)* The afternoon it was raining?

TEACHER   Yes.

BOY   There was a storm, sir. It started all of a sudden. We were in a room.

TEACHER   Which room? With whom?

BOY   He's very nice, sir.

TEACHER   Who is?

BOY   I was going to be late for school. He said: "People are bad. You can't trust anyone. Put on your raincoat. Let's go." *(pause)* We'd been there a long time.

TEACHER   Where is this place?

BOY   He's very nice. I like him a lot.

TEACHER   Who is he?

BOY   I remember the first time I saw him. I was at the National Park, studying with a friend. He was there, too, sitting on the bench across from us. There was a gravel road in between and people were passing by. Beside him—beside his bench—there was a drinking fountain. I didn't see him 'til I went to get a drink. I was thirsty. I saw that he was smiling at me and I smiled, too. Then I went back to study and I forgot all about him. I totally forgot.

TEACHER   Then?

BOY   It was getting dark. We were getting ready to leave when I saw him again. He was still sitting on the bench. He'd been there the whole time and I didn't notice. He smiled at me and I smiled back. As I walked away, I turned 'round and smiled again. I don't know why I liked him.

TEACHER   Had anyone else wanted to be your friend before this?

BOY   No, sir. *(pause)* We were in a room. There was hardly a cloud in the sky, then suddenly there was thunder and lightning. It was a storm. He said he'd walk with me to school. We left his house and he said: "Don't be afraid! What are you afraid of? They can't see us. Look! There are so many trees separating them from us, so many clouds, many mountains, so many people."

TEACHER   What's his name? Who is he?

BOY   I go to his house, sir. We talk about everything. We plant flowers in the garden and cut the weeds. We sit in the sun and eat together.

TEACHER   What else?

BOY   What else? He reads me books. He has lots of books.

TEACHER   What kind of books?

BOY   Stories... fiction.

TEACHER   Such as?

BOY   Such as... the story of the prince who wanted to steal a flower from an enchanted castle. Do you know that story?

TEACHER   No.

BOY   Or the one about the boy kept in a tower by a witch's spell?

TEACHER   How often do you go there?

BOY   Whenever I can. Sometimes I tell my parents I'm going to see a movie, but I go there.

TEACHER   You lie to your parents?

BOY   What should I tell them?

TEACHER   Why don't you tell them the truth?

BOY   The truth about what?

TEACHER   About where you go.

BOY   I don't know.

TEACHER   Because you're doing something very wrong and you're afraid. You don't tell them because you're afraid.

BOY   I don't do anything wrong, sir.

TEACHER   *(harshly)* Shut up! *(silence)* If your parents found out about this they would kill you. You would be publicly disgraced, as you've been in this school. Don't you realize what they're saying behind your back? How do you think I've found out about this?

BOY   I just told you, sir.

   Silence.

TEACHER   Why did you go to his house?

BOY   He asked me to, sir. We came out of the movie theatre and as we were walking down the street, he said: "Let's go to my place." I asked him: "Why can't the prince steal the flower from that enchanted castle?" He laughed and said: "Why can't the boy in the tower escape that witch"? Then we went to his house.

TEACHER   The very first time you saw him?

BOY   No, sir. It was a few days later. He said, "Let's go to my place and talk."

TEACHER   And you went with him?

BOY   Yes, sir. You can't imagine how beautiful his house is.

TEACHER   Besides reading books and planting flowers, what else do you do there?

BOY   He likes me a lot, sir. His eyes are full of kindness when he looks at me. Once there were tears in his eyes and his lips were trembling. He held my face in his hands and caressed it over and over. I touched his face, too. He said: "You smell of life, of wind and cloud. Do you understand what I'm saying?" Is it all right that I'm telling you this, sir?

TEACHER   Yes, go on.

   From here on in, the TEACHER's walk, which has been in a straight line in front of the BOY, becomes a steady circle. His walking must be as slow as possible, so that at a glance we don't see him move.

BOY   When I'm tired, I lay my head on his lap and sleep. Once I had a dream—

TEACHER   You haven't told me his name.

BOY   He asked me not to tell. He asked me not to tell anyone that we're friends, that we know each other. Because people wouldn't understand.

TEACHER   But you can tell me.

BOY   Should I tell you about the dream I had?

TEACHER   Dream?

> *It seems like he is remembering something. From here on he becomes more and more internal.*

BOY   I dreamt we were lying in a meadow. The weather was beautiful. The air was sweet. He told me…

TEACHER   "People are not nice. You can't trust anyone."

BOY   The clouds are magical. I said: "I love you so much."

TEACHER   *(gently)* So do I.

BOY   In the distance teachers and students were passing by as if they couldn't see us. My parents were there, too, talking by themselves. They couldn't see us either. But then I was scared. I was trembling.

TEACHER   Don't be afraid! What are you afraid of? They won't see. Look! There are so many trees separating them from us, so many clouds, many mountains, so many people.

BOY   I'm not scared. The wind made me shiver.

TEACHER   Come into my arms.

BOY   You're so warm.

TEACHER   It's the weather.

BOY   And then we were under the earth, buried up to our necks. Something was pulling on our heads. They were being torn from our shoulders—only a few strands held them in place—and the space in between was filling with clay. I was terrified. I thought that any second my head would fly from my body and I would die. I said: "I'm freezing to death." He said: "Let's go to my house."

TEACHER   Let's go to my house.

BOY   I turned around to tell him something, but he wasn't facing me anymore. I could only see his back, his hair. Then it got sunny. It got very hot. I found myself sitting in class, talking to you. You said: "Wait! Sit down!" I said: "Yes, sir." You said: "You smell of life, of wind and clouds. Do you understand what I'm saying?" I said: "No, sir."

> *A long silence.*

TEACHER   Would you like to have dinner with me?

BOY Yes, sir.

TEACHER It wouldn't be too late for you?

BOY No, sir.

TEACHER We'll throw a big party then. Make dinner together and eat it, just the two of us.

BOY What about the boy in the tower?

TEACHER He has to stay in there, but we can invite the witch.

The TEACHER caresses the BOY's head. The lights snap out.

THE FIFTH FOLD

<u>Star Rains, Black</u>

A desert. The earth is covered with rocks and gravel. A well, centre stage. HAMON and MO are anxiously pacing and waiting for someone. Once in a while the sound of cars is heard in the distance. It's night. The moon and stars are out. The reflection of a light coming out of the well illuminates the stage. This is the only light required for this act.

HAMON What time is it? *(pause)* They should be here any minute now.

MO I doubt it.

HAMON What?

MO Doesn't look good. Maybe they couldn't do it.

HAMON Who told you about this well?

MO This thing? You did, didn't you?

HAMON When?

MO When?!

Freeze. They look at each other. MO kicks a rock into the well. There is no sound. They pace.

Have you met these two before?

HAMON Who?

MO The clients.

HAMON Fucknuts! How d'you think I made the deal with them!?

MO *(with joy)* Crackle, crackle, crackle!

HAMON What?

MO How they going to get him to come here?

HAMON Sex.

MO In the desert? Do they have a car?

HAMON I don't know. They have to get here somehow, don't they?

MO Get where? (*They look at each other in silence. They pace.*) You're afraid.

        HAMON stops and looks at him. Silence. They pace.

You think they got the guts?

HAMON Doesn't take guts.

MO Sure it does. (*pause*) You haven't told me the plan yet.

HAMON Plan? Bash him over the head with a rock and chuck him in the well.

MO We should hide ourselves somewhere.

HAMON We wait 'til they show up.

MO What if we get blood on us?

HAMON What?

MO Well, what are we gonna do?

        The lights go to black for a second and come back. HAMON is not there.

We shouldn't have agreed to this. (*pause*) What if we get caught? We won't. What if a cop follows them? Jackoff, you think they won't recognize his hat? What about the guy?

        The lights go to black for a second and then come up. HAMON is standing in the same place as before. Silence. MO takes out a small pocket radio and turns it on. He finds a station. They stand motionless and listen.

FIRST WOMAN (*voice-over*) Why not?

SECOND WOMAN (*voice-over*) We'll be caught.

FIRST WOMAN (*voice-over*) No.

SECOND WOMAN (*voice-over*) We'll be caught and put away.

FIRST WOMAN (*voice-over*) We'll throw him in a ditch.

SECOND WOMAN (*voice-over*) He's heavy. He's too heavy.

FIRST WOMAN (*voice-over*) Well, both of us will—

SECOND WOMAN (*voice-over*) I'm scared. I won't touch him.

FIRST WOMAN (*voice-over*) Shut up.

SECOND WOMAN   *(voice-over)* I won't touch a dead man. I won't.

FIRST WOMAN   *(voice-over)* Pee-ewe!

SECOND WOMAN   *(voice-over)* I'm gonna barf.

FIRST WOMAN   *(voice-over)* Hold it back.

SECOND WOMAN   *(voice-over)* I can't.

> *Silence. MO changes the station. Coughing. Pause.*

MAN   *(voice-over)* Here is perfect. No one can see us.

FIRST WOMAN   *(voice-over)* No, let's go a bit further.

MAN   *(voice-over)* What's wrong with here?

SECOND WOMAN   *(voice-over)* Let's go behind that hill.

HAMON   Jesus H. Christ! What the hell is that? Turn it off.

MO   *(turning it off)* It's a story, a drama.

HAMON   I'm tired of walking.

MO   *(warning)* Don't sit.

HAMON   Why not?

MO   Shake off your coat! It's dusty.

HAMON   I feel much better now.

MO   Remember, we haven't seen each other today.

HAMON   Right. There better not be any hassle.

MO   There won't be. Just act like nothing happened.

HAMON   I feel much better now. *(pause)* Exactly why is it I can't sit?

MO   Because you'll mess up your clothes. We should never have agreed to this. It's always the same thing every time.

HAMON   They'll get here.

MO   And if they don't.

HAMON   The better for us, we'll take off then.

MO   Wasn't it you who said they'd show up any minute?

HAMON   I'm not the All-Omnipotent. Maybe something went wrong.

MO   I say we torch him.

HAMON   Shut up.

MO   He'll burn, fizzle, sizzle. He'll crack, crunch, crunch, crunch.

HAMON   Are you completely nuts?

MO   What difference would it make to him?

HAMON   Well, what about the client?

MO   They just want him dead. They don't care how.

HAMON   The well. Only the well.

MO   Give me some of your bread.

HAMON   *(pointing to his pocket)* It's been there since yesterday.

MO   That's all right. *(HAMON takes a piece of bread out of his pocket and breaks it into halves. They eat quickly and nervously while talking.)* You're scared.

HAMON   Bullshit!

MO   You're scared.

HAMON   Get lost!

MO   You're scared.

HAMON   Get lost, I said!

MO   Tell me the story then.

HAMON   I hit him on the chest, in the gut, on the face, the motherfucker. I was out of breath. I didn't know what else to do. He said: "Someone's laughing at us." I said: "I wish we had some vodka." Someone's laughing.

> *A dog barks in the distance.*

MO   Want some vodka?

HAMON   Anything left?

MO   'Bout half.

HAMON   Ah, why not? The night is young.

> *MO takes a bottle of vodka out of his pocket, opens it and offers it to HAMON.*

MO   Bottoms up!

HAMON   After you!

> *MO drinks and passes the bottle to HAMON. From here on, the bottle goes hand to hand between them 'til it's finished.*

HAMON   Fucker! I've got nothing to go with it.

MO   You want pretzels?

HAMON   You got pretzels?

MO I'll go get some at the corner.

HAMON Don't screw around. I'm not in the mood.

MO I'm serious.

HAMON I said don't fuck with me, asshole!

> *Silence.*

MO Let's get out of here!

> *Silence.*

Well?

HAMON I don't know.

MO Just what is it we're waiting for?

HAMON Turn on the radio.

MO Come on, we'll listen to it on the way back.

HAMON I say we wait.

MO Ahhh!

> *MO throws the bottle away. He takes the radio out of his pocket and turns it on. They stand motionless and listen.*

BOY *(voice-over)* I remember the first time I saw him. I was at the National Park, studying with a friend. He was there, too, sitting on a bench across from us. There was a gravel road between us and people were passing by. Beside him— beside his bench—there was a drinking fountain. I didn't see him 'til I went to get a drink. I was thirsty. I saw that he was smiling at me and I smiled, too. Then I went back to study and I forgot all about him. I totally forgot.

MO What is this crap?

HAMON How am I supposed to know?

MO Turn it off?

HAMON No!

> *MO turns off the radio and puts it back into his pocket. A dog is barking in the distance. Pause. The light goes to black for a second and comes back up. MO is not there. From here on HAMON looks, speaks and walks as if someone is beside him.*

Let's go. How can they get here without a car? *(looking into the distance)* Is that them? Not a chance! How could they walk here? What if they come when we've gone? What's going to happen to them? I don't like this. Well we could hang out longer if you want. No, let's go! If they were going to come they would be here by now. Maybe they took care of it themselves, and we've been wasting our time. Yeah, maybe they're somewhere fucking him in the sand. Shit, I'm getting pissed. Thank God we had some vodka. Yeah, that was all right. *(pause)* Go then? *(pause)* No, fuck 'em all. What for? Were they here yesterday? The day before yesterday? The day before that? *(pause)* Tomorrow? Forget it, let's go.

> HAMON *exits stage left. Silence. A moment later, a dusty man drags himself out of the well. A dog barks. The light in the well goes off. The moon goes off. The stars, one by one, turn off.*

Interrogation

Mohammad Rahmanian
Translated by Soheil Parsa

Ali Momen
photo by Setareh Delzendeh

Michelle Latimer
photo by Setareh Delzendeh

Interrogation was first presented as a workshop production at the SummerWorks Festival 2006, Toronto from August 3 to August 13 with the following company:

NAEEM	Ali Momen
VOICE of male interrogator	Earl Pastko
SAFIYA	Michelle Latimer
VOICE of female interrogator	Leanna Brodie

Director: Soheil Parsa
Stage Manager: Brenda Kamino
Costume Design: The Cast
Sound Designer: Thomas Payne
Producer: Julianne Baragar

• • •

Awards and Nominations
Best Direction and Best Ensemble (Best of SummerWorks, *NOW* Magazine).

First Episode – Killing Monsieur Fonton's Cat

Characters

NAEEM, an Algerian teenager
VOICE, a male interrogator

Time

1964

Place

Algeria

Second Episode – Stop Calling Me, Mother!

Characters

SAFIYA, a twenty-nine-year-old Algerian woman
VOICE, a female interrogator

Time

1964

Place

Algeria

Interrogation

A Play in Two Episodes

FIRST EPISODE

<u>Killing Monsieur Fonton's Cat</u>

Blackout. A combination of different sounds on radio frequencies: the voice of a reporter in Arabic, French music, the siren of an ambulance, the sound of a public demonstration, Arabic music, the sounds of machine guns, the voice of a French reporter. All of a sudden a single intense light snaps in, revealing NAEEM, an Algerian teenage boy. He is in grey pyjamas, sitting on a chair. His hair is dishevelled. He suffers from a mental disorder. The VOICE of a male interrogator is talking to him.

VOICE   Move your hand.

NAEEM   It's too bright. Hurts my eyes.

VOICE   You'll get used to it.

NAEEM   I can't see you.

VOICE   It doesn't matter. I'm a person just like you.

NAEEM   You sound like Farhat.

VOICE   Farhat?

NAEEM   He's wicked. *(indicating with his hands)* Has a slingshot this big. In the evenings he goes after the crows… poor creatures! I hate him.

VOICE   Why? Because he kills the crows?

NAEEM   Because he won't give me his slingshot… he has a thick voice like you.

VOICE   Do you hate me?

NAEEM   Do you have a moustache?

VOICE   Yes.

NAEEM   Okay. *(Silence. He gazes at the floor.)*

VOICE   Can you tell me your name?

NAEEM   Yep.

VOICE   Well?

NAEEM   Is it really hard to shoot a crow while it's flying fast? Do you know how to?

VOICE   I don't. I've never tried.

NAEEM   Gosh, there are so many hard things to do in this world.

VOICE   Such as?

NAEEM   Singing a nice song. Leaping over a ditch. Twisting the handlebars of Mr. Fonton's moustache…

VOICE   Have you ever done a difficult thing?

NAEEM   Once I glued Nafisa's rooster's ass shut.

VOICE   Then what happened?

NAEEM   Couldn't crow anymore.

VOICE   Then? What happened then?

NAEEM   *(laughs)* It died…. If cocks can't crow, they die.

VOICE   No one noticed? No one punished you?

NAEEM   You and God are the only ones that know.

VOICE   Aren't you afraid that I'll tell Nafisa what you did to her rooster?

>   *NAEEM gazes at the light in silence.*

NAEEM   Naeem.

VOICE   What?

NAEEM   My name's Naeem.

VOICE   How old are you Naeem?

NAEEM   Me? Eighteen. But I'm very strong, much stronger than Monique, who was one year older than me.

VOICE   Her name was Monique?

NAEEM   Yeah… that shit.

VOICE   What was her last name?

NAEEM   Fournier… Monique Fournier, the French shit. She was totally scared of me. You know why? Because I was stronger than her.

VOICE   Was she your friend?

NAEEM   How can you be friends with a pig? Especially a French pig.

VOICE   Was she your enemy?

NAEEM   The enemy of our whatchamacallit… *(searches for the right word)* …the enemy of our nation.

VOICE   A nineteen-year-old girl?

NAEEM   She was lying when she said she was nineteen… with her height, she must have been a hundred years old… the tall, French shit…

VOICE   Who told you that Monique Fournier was the enemy of your nation?

NAEEM   Jamila.

VOICE   Who is she?

NAEEM   One of those you might call a sister.

VOICE   Your sister?

NAEEM   Yep.

VOICE   How old is she?

NAEEM   Fifteen. She's fifteen but the way she talks you'd think she's sixteen.

VOICE   Did she ask you to do it?

NAEEM   She has lots of hair. When she braids her hair, she becomes so beautiful. Exactly like the photo I put on our toilet wall. Why don't your toilets here have any photos?

VOICE   If you answer my questions properly, I'll give you a beautiful photo.

NAEEM   Oh yeah? *(sarcastically)* Do you own a photo gallery or something?

VOICE   No, but for you…

NAEEM   She deserved it.

VOICE   Who?

NAEEM   Monique… I always wanted to pull her blond hair.

VOICE   What role did Jamila play in what you did?

NAEEM   Why? If you have a moustache is it your sister's fault?

VOICE   I don't understand! No, it's not my sister's fault that I have a moustache.

NAEEM   That's right… a sister is a sister.

VOICE   Do you hate men with moustaches?

NAEEM   Nope.

VOICE   Then why do you constantly talk about moustaches? Why do you have a moustache yourself?

NAEEM   I'm afraid.

VOICE   Of what?

NAEEM   Because a crow with a wounded wing can't fly very far.

VOICE   What?

NAEEM Like a sparrow whose eyes are plucked out, it hits the first tree that comes across its path and falls dead.

VOICE Naeem...

NAEEM But they say that blind hunting dogs find the prey faster, because their sense of smell gets sharper...

VOICE Naeem, Naeem... focus.

NAEEM ...Ha?

VOICE Are you all right?

NAEEM A bunch of bees are stinging in my head...

VOICE Do you want to say something?

NAEEM Yes.

VOICE What? What would you like to say?

NAEEM I want to count my fingers.

VOICE So do it.

NAEEM Nope.

VOICE Why not?

NAEEM Because I know how many there are... ten. It's really boring if one knows how many fingers he has? Isn't it?

VOICE Yes...

NAEEM My dad's lucky.

VOICE Why? He doesn't know how to count?

NAEEM He has nine toes... his right leg is shorter. But no one knows about it. If he hits me again, I'll go and tell the whole neighbourhood. Then he'll chase after me with his short leg, but he won't be able to catch me.

VOICE What's his name?

NAEEM Is it a good thing if one knows everyone's name in this world?

VOICE I don't know.

NAEEM It must be really fun, eh?

VOICE Maybe.

NAEEM If I tell you a secret you won't tell anyone?

VOICE No.

NAEEM I know the names of every Arab in our neighbourhood.

VOICE   Bravo.

NAEEM   They call me "Son of Saleem, the Short Leg."

VOICE   Your father, this "Saleem, the Short Leg," what does he do for a living?

NAEEM   He's… a thing… a smuggler.

VOICE   What does he smuggle?

NAEEM   Everything. Camel cigarettes, fabric, British tobacco. He takes goods from Oja to Telsman.

VOICE   How do you know all of this?

NAEEM   Sometimes I go with him.

VOICE   Do you know that smuggling is a crime?

NAEEM   What does crime mean?

VOICE   It means wrongdoing.

NAEEM   My dad says that's bullshit. Of course he doesn't say bullshit. He uses a very bad word that Jamila asked me not to tell anyone.

VOICE   Even me?

NAEEM   Nope.

VOICE   Why not?

NAEEM   If I don't tell you, will you whip me?

VOICE   No.

NAEEM   Why? Have you lost your belt?

VOICE   No. Even if I had one, I wouldn't.

NAEEM   Can you draw flowers?

VOICE   What?

NAEEM   A flower with four red petals?

VOICE   Yes, I think so.

NAEEM   I had a teacher. She once drew a beautiful flower on the back of my notebook. She liked me a lot. She never got mad at me. *(silence)*

VOICE   Then?

NAEEM   Then she died like Mr. Fonton's dirty cat.

VOICE   How?

NAEEM   The French did something to my teacher and she threw herself under a train. People said she became a bride.

VOICE   Was she deflowered?

NAEEM   I don't know. Does it hurt? She screamed so much. The top of her stocking was torn.

VOICE   And what did you do?

NAEEM   Waited.

VOICE   For what?

NAEEM   To grow up.

VOICE   So you could do what?

NAEEM   Go on the streets and yell, "Down with the French!"

VOICE   But Naeem…

NAEEM   Jamila used to put my head on her lap and say, "Naeem, why have you grown up so late?"

VOICE   She loves you?

NAEEM   Hope she finds a strong husband.

VOICE   Why?

NAEEM   Those fucking liars say I tossed Mr. Fonton's cat under the train.

VOICE   Are they right?

NAEEM   I love cats so much.

VOICE   Why?

NAEEM   Aren't they human beings?

VOICE   Do you like human beings?

NAEEM   More then beef patties.

VOICE   Then why did you do it?

NAEEM   What was the revolution for?

VOICE   But Naeem, the revolution is over. We won. We kicked the French out of our country…

NAEEM   Not all of them. Monique and her father were still there.

VOICE   But they weren't supporting the imperialists. Do you know what imperialism means?

    NAEEM nods.

Well, what does it mean?

NAEEM   Means motherfucker bastard shit.

VOICE Do you know what you did was a great sin?

NAEEM My dad used to show me his four-toed foot saying, "Sin means this." Then he put his dentures in his mouth and bit me.

VOICE Why?

NAEEM Because he had lost all his teeth.

VOICE Naeem, why did you take Monique to that quiet street?

NAEEM Then the princess held the prince's hand and they lived together happily ever after.

VOICE What are you talking about?

NAEEM This is the end of the story. Beautiful, isn't it?

VOICE Yes. But it's a lie.

NAEEM That's why I took her to that back alley.

VOICE Go on, Naeem. I'm listening.

NAEEM Hunters kill the dogs if they don't…

VOICE You were talking about Monique.

NAEEM I pulled up my moustache and said, "Look, I'm harelipped… are you"?

VOICE Me?

NAEEM When you were a child how did you hide your harelip?

VOICE I'm not harelipped.

NAEEM Then why do you have a moustache? Behind it is a drooling hole. I'm scared.

VOICE I assure you that my lips are totally fine.

NAEEM A crow is already a shitty bird. It'll be shittier when one of its wings is broken.

VOICE Yes, you're correct.

NAEEM Are you big enough to snatch Farhat's slingshot from him and give it to me?

VOICE What do you need it for?

NAEEM I took it to my room. Tried to fix its wing. But it couldn't fly. It felt too lonely.

VOICE Do you know what loneliness means?

NAEEM Of course I do.

VOICE What does it mean?

NAEEM It's like a thumb in the mouth.

VOICE Explain.

NAEEM ...Like the sky above my head... or exactly like God.

VOICE Would you like to tell me what happened on that day, in that remote neighbourhood, at the end of Tanoor Street?

NAEEM What day?

VOICE September 17th, 1962.

NAEEM Was it a Tuesday?

VOICE Friday.

NAEEM Sure. *(silence)*

VOICE You don't want to talk?

NAEEM *(quickly, non-stop)* Colonization, corruption, history, minority, society, land, homeland, occupation, revolution, freedom, conspiracy, terror, traitors, terrorist, machine guns...

VOICE Naeem, Naeem. Calm down.

NAEEM *(calmly)* Learned them all from the radio. I know so many other things.

VOICE Friday evening, at exactly seven-thirty, September 17th, 1962, what were you thinking about?

NAEEM About my drawing book.

VOICE Why your drawing book?

NAEEM Only three blank pages left.

VOICE What did you wish to draw on them?

NAEEM *(after a moment)* It's full of beautiful pictures... airplanes, machine guns, tanks; the people who have been shot by French soldiers...

VOICE On the remaining pages, do you still want to draw machine guns?

NAEEM If someone lies, does he go to hell?

VOICE I believe so.

NAEEM Why?

VOICE I don't know. Why? Have you ever lied?

NAEEM Do they let tall people into hell?

VOICE They let everyone in.

NAEEM   Then Monique Fournier goes to hell big time.

VOICE   Was she a liar?

NAEEM   She'll burn…. Her blond hair…

VOICE   Why?

NAEEM   Do you know a story that has a real ending?

VOICE   Yes, I do, Naeem…

NAEEM   She said, "I don't mind harelipped guys."

VOICE   Who? Monique said that?

NAEEM   Do you think on Fridays they go to parties, too?

VOICE   Who?

NAEEM   The crows. There wasn't a single crow on that deserted street…. She was wearing the same skirt.

VOICE   Which one?

NAEEM   The one that when she was spinning, I could see her whole body. The red one.

VOICE   You didn't like that skirt?

NAEEM   Once she danced at my cousin's wedding…

VOICE   Did you like it?

NAEEM   I was looking down counting my toes. Do you have ten toes, too?

VOICE   Yes. You were saying about that Friday evening, in that back alley.

NAEEM   Are you a cop?

VOICE   No

NAEEM   Do you think that I threw Mr. Fonton's cat under the train?

VOICE   I don't know. Did you?

NAEEM   During the revolution, did any cats get shot?

VOICE   Yes. Possibly.

NAEEM   Of course. It's a revolution. Everyone gets shot, even the cats. I keep asking my dad to tell me about the revolution.

VOICE   Does he tell you?

NAEEM   He says revolution is bullshit.

VOICE   Explain that.

NAEEM He says revolution is just for fooling some coo-coo brains like me. Of course he doesn't say coo-coo brains. He uses a very bad word that Jamila asked me not to tell anyone.

VOICE So, your father is an anti-revolutionary?

NAEEM No. Come on. This is Saleem, Saleem the short leg. Have you forgotten?

VOICE No, I haven't.

NAEEM If I tell you a secret you won't tell anyone?

VOICE No. I promise.

NAEEM Jamila wants to chop his head off.

VOICE Your father's head?

NAEEM One night when he's asleep. Then his radio will be mine.

VOICE When did Jamila tell you this?

NAEEM It takes only one battery, this big. But you can reach the whole world with it.

VOICE What else has Jamila told you?

NAEEM She said, "Naeem, wait 'til I get my allowance from my father. Then Jamila won't have to cut your dad's throat."

VOICE Who said that to you? Monique?

NAEEM She'll burn. She'll burn.

VOICE Monique? What else did she tell you?

NAEEM Have I done anything to you?

VOICE No, you haven't.

NAEEM Then why are you bugging me just like those kids from Tanoor Street?

VOICE We want to help you.

NAEEM I don't need any help. I want my drawing book.

VOICE I'll find it for you. Promise.

NAEEM The last three pages are blank.

VOICE I know.

NAEEM I didn't draw anyone's picture in it.

VOICE Naeem, when did you decide to do it?

NAEEM I didn't decide. I held her hand. I thought it would smell of perfume.

VOICE Didn't it?

NAEEM   It smelled of coffee. Do you like coffee?

VOICE   Yes, I do.

NAEEM   Her eyes were shining like a cat's…

VOICE   Continue.

NAEEM   Sure. *(silence)*

VOICE   I said continue.

NAEEM   Did you say that you weren't a cop?

VOICE   Yes, I did. But you must tell me the rest of…

NAEEM   Did I tell you about the crow with a broken wing?

VOICE   Yes, yes. You've told me already.

NAEEM   Then what else is there to say?

VOICE   What I want from you is this: on Friday evening, September 17th, 1962, you lured Monique Fournier, the nineteen-year-old daughter of Roger Fournier, the construction worker, to a remote neighbourhood beyond Tanoor Street and…

NAEEM   Once we had a neighbour who had a cart…

VOICE   Naeem, Naeem… answer me.

NAEEM   The sky was blue…

VOICE   I'm talking to you. Listen to me.

NAEEM   Eeny meeny miney mo, catch the tiger by the toe, if it…

VOICE   What did Monique Fournier tell you?

NAEEM   *(taunting)* If you tell dirty jokes, I'm gonna tell on you…

VOICE   Monique Fournier, Naeem. That tall French girl…

NAEEM   *(calling)* Jamila! This guy just said "Son of a fuck, bitch…"

VOICE   What did you do to that girl?

NAEEM   He says, gluing up the ass of a…

VOICE   What did she tell you?

NAEEM   This Monique keeps putting her hand on my shoulder.

VOICE   Did she love you?

NAEEM   She says, "Hey, good-looking, you wanna marry me?"

VOICE   What else did she tell you?

NAEEM   Can I tell you a joke?

VOICE   Why did you do that?

NAEEM   I can whistle, too, walk on my hands…

VOICE   Why Naeem?

NAEEM   Why should one go to hell just for a white lie?

VOICE   Why did you do that to her?

NAEEM   *(calmly)* If I tell you, you won't tell anyone?

VOICE   No, I promise.

NAEEM   I'll burn in the fire of hell like Monique.

VOICE   Why?

NAEEM   The last three pages of my drawing book aren't blank. I've drawn pictures on them.

VOICE   What pictures?

NAEEM   First the sky was blue, very blue, like a morning dream. I said, "Look, I'm harelipped… aren't you scared of me?" There was the smell of coffee. She said, "No, I'm not scared of you." She didn't know that the tall people would be let into hell too. I wanted to tell her the story of my crow. She said, "Hey good-looking, you wanna marry me?" I wished I could look down and count my toes. But I knew there were ten. Always ten. Never happened to be nine or eleven. I thought someone was behind the wall, on Tanoor Street. "What if it's Jamila?" I opened my mouth to say, "Down with the French," but I said…

VOICE   What did you say?

NAEEM   I said…

VOICE   What? Say it Naeem. What did you say?

NAEEM   "I love you." *(weeps in silence)*

VOICE   And then what happened?

NAEEM   And then the sky started spinning. It was no longer blue. I looked at her. It wasn't only her skirt that was red. Her whole body, all her clothes were red.

VOICE   Why did you kill her?

NAEEM   Because she couldn't fly anymore. I tried to fix her broken wing. But it didn't work.

VOICE   She loved you, Naeem, do you understand?

NAEEM   One who knows all the jokes of the world, nothing can make him laugh.

VOICE   If she would have come back to life, come to you. Would you stay with her?

NAEEM   *(He takes a piece of paper out of his pocket. It's a drawing of a girl.)* At night, I stick it on the wall above my head… you won't tell Jamila?

VOICE   No, I won't.

NAEEM   Do you know what death means?

VOICE   Do you?

NAEEM   Means your heart bleeds and you go to God. If you go to God you'll never return.

VOICE   Do you want anything?

NAEEM   Yes. A razor.

VOICE   What for?

NAEEM   To shave my moustache. I don't need it anymore.

VOICE   Sure. I'll bring one for you.

NAEEM   One more thing.

VOICE   Go on, I'm listening.

NAEEM   Promise?

VOICE   Yes.

NAEEM   I didn't kill Mr. Fonton's cat.

>   *Light snaps out. A combination of various sounds on radio frequencies; the voice of reporters in different languages, sound of a public demonstration, machine guns…*

>   *End of First Episode.*

SECOND EPISODE

<u>Stop Calling Me, Mother!</u>

Blackout. The sound of a memorable French song from a gramophone, the sound of an explosion, screaming of the crowd, police and ambulance sirens, again the same French song. All of a sudden a single intense light snaps in, revealing SAFIYA. She is sitting on a chair, staring wide-eyed in front of her. The VOICE of a female interrogator is talking to her.

VOICE   You still don't want to sleep?

SAFIYA   *(with a choked voice)* No.

VOICE   You haven't slept for seventy-two hours.

SAFIYA   Seventy-six.

VOICE   And you don't feel tired at all!

SAFIYA   Yes, I do… I'm tired. Very tired.

VOICE   Then why don't you sleep? Is this another kind of protest?

SAFIYA   You…. Your voice is too loud.

VOICE   Does it bother you?

SAFIYA   My ears… my ears are damaged.

VOICE   Why?

SAFIYA   It's in my file.

VOICE   Let me see. *(the sound of turning pages)*

SAFIYA   *(angrily, but still in a choked voice)* Stop that noise.

VOICE   Are you all right?

SAFIYA   *(calmly)* Yes, I am.

VOICE   Can you introduce yourself?

SAFIYA   It's in my file. First and last name, father's name and so on.

VOICE   I know. But we would like to hear it from you.

SAFIYA   *(shocked)* We…? How many are you? Five? Six?

VOICE   Does it matter?

SAFIYA   There were usually five. An inspector, an interrogator, the man with the rubber cord and two others in grey.

VOICE   Grey?

SAFIYA   The interrogator's assistants. All together they were five. But that day one more was added to the team.

VOICE   This is related to your time served in the Barbarous Prison before the revolution, isn't it?

SAFIYA   Why, in the ID forms, is there no mention of a mother? It's always first name, last name and father's name…

VOICE   Well, that's the tradition.

SAFIYA   Many Kasbah residents don't know their father's names. Mostly those of mixed-blood.

VOICE   That's true. Statistics show that rape rates by the French in that region were pretty high.

SAFIYA   My mother knew more than twenty lullabies.

VOICE   You still don't want to tell me your name?

SAFIYA   Prisoner number 2268. Algeria, August 10th, 1959.

VOICE   Right. Notice the date you just mentioned. August 1959. And now it is 1964. The number belongs to the period of your incarceration before the revolution.

SAFIYA   I haven't been given a number here yet. They were more organized in those days.

VOICE   But we're not talking to you as a prisoner here. This is an interview, not an interrogation.

SAFIYA   Then it's possible to write in the ID form, "Name: Safiya. Last Name: Larosi. Father's name…," no, "Mother's name: Neja…"

VOICE   Neja Hanshi…. Correct?

SAFIYA   Did you know her?

VOICE   There's some info about her in your file.

SAFIYA   She was loud like you.

VOICE   You're very sensitive to sound, aren't you?

SAFIYA   First time that I was thrown to the French jail, I was sixteen…

VOICE   Go on.

SAFIYA   Ah, never mind… forget about it. Do you have a cigarette?

VOICE   I'm sorry. It's not permitted here.

SAFIYA   Yeah, not allowed, prohibited. As my German fluid mechanics prof used to say "*Verboten.*"

VOICE   How did you get interested in physics?

SAFIYA   Well, NLF had different branches. Do you know what NLF is?

VOICE   I believe it stands for National Liberation Front of Algeria.

SAFIYA   That's the one. I wasn't strong enough to carry a machine gun or… throw a hand grenade like this. *(demonstrates)* That's why… *(suddenly)* Yes?

VOICE   What?

SAFIYA   Did someone call me?

VOICE   I don't think so.

SAFIYA   I heard my mother.

VOICE   No one called you, Safiya.

SAFIYA   What's your name?

VOICE   Why are you asking?

SAFIYA   You call me by my name. But I don't know yours. This is…. How do you say… not fair.

VOICE   Does it make any difference if you know my name?

SAFIYA   No, not really…. Are you married?

VOICE   Yes.

SAFIYA   Children?

VOICE   A boy.

SAFIYA   What's his name.

VOICE   His father is French. He chose his name.

SAFIYA   What?

VOICE   Camon.

SAFIYA   Camon! Beautiful. It's the name of a spice in Arabic. A local spice…

VOICE   Interesting. I didn't know that.

SAFIYA   Do you know what I wish?

VOICE   What?

SAFIYA   I wish I could yawn.

VOICE   So do it.

SAFIYA   I'm afraid to hear the routine questions again, "You wanna sleep? You don't wanna sleep? Haven't slept for days…? Is this a kind of protest?"

VOICE   Well isn't it?

SAFIYA   What?

VOICE   A protest.

SAFIYA   Protest is a kind of opposition. And I don't oppose anything anymore.

VOICE   Seriously?

SAFIYA   Seriously.

VOICE   Not even your arrest?

SAFIYA   I've been arrested many times. This is the fourth time.

VOICE   This time is different. Before, you were arrested by the enemies of the revolution, but this time…

SAFIYA   All jails are the same. They just have different names. I've been to Barbarous Prison as well as Hussein D Jail. You think it's possible to solve an equation on the walls of Al-byar Prison?

VOICE   What equation?

SAFIYA   The dynamic equation. *(recites without pausing)*

$$M(t) \frac{dv(t)}{dt} = F \text{ ext} + \frac{dm(t)}{dt}$$

VOICE   Hold on, Safiya… calm down.

SAFIYA   *(frightened)* Was I too loud?

VOICE   No, you were talking too fast.

SAFIYA   If I get too loud, let me know. All right?

VOICE   I will. What are you afraid of?

SAFIYA   I've told her a hundred times "Mother, stop calling me. At least don't call me so loudly!"

VOICE   But she didn't listen. Correct?

SAFIYA   Have you ever foamed?

VOICE   Foamed?

SAFIYA   Yes, foamed.

VOICE   Is that an expression?

SAFIYA   No, it's not. One can really foam. Like soap with big and tiny bubbles…

VOICE   Never heard of it.

SAFIYA   Is there anything in my file about this?

VOICE   No, I haven't come across anything like it.

SAFIYA   You're right. They don't write these things in the files. Only first name, last name, father's name… without mother's name.

VOICE   Speaking of files, I think we should take a look at yours. Should we? *(silence)* The incident took place on a Sunday, at exactly 10:00 a.m. Correct?

SAFIYA   Incorrect. I've never made time bombs. My expertise lies elsewhere.

VOICE   Where?

SAFIYA   *(after a short pause)* Where do you usually go on Sundays? Let me try. *(thinks)* To the beach, right?

VOICE   Well… yes, sometimes.

SAFIYA   Sandcastles… children play with the shovels and buckets… God… *(suddenly)* Yes, Mother?

VOICE   No one called you, Safiya.

SAFIYA   Child, child, child. She wanted a child for me and a grandson for herself.

VOICE   Do you have siblings?

SAFIYA   I had a brother. *(silence)*

VOICE   Had?

SAFIYA   In 1960, he was killed in Mostaghanem.

VOICE   Was he a fighter?

SAFIYA   I don't know. I was in prison at the time. Have you ever been to Mostaghanem?

VOICE   Once I drove through the city. There were big gaps between the French and the Arabs. I believe this has been resolved since the revolution.

SAFIYA   A hundred more revolutions won't be able to solve these gaps. Because they aren't political; they're geographical. There is a huge gap between the French and the Arabs.

VOICE   Good ones on one side and the bad ones on the other.

SAFIYA   Depends what you mean by good and bad… I had my training there.

VOICE   Military training?

SAFIYA   I've told you once that I wasn't a machine gun or grenade person. I was associated with the engineering unit, the destruction squad.

VOICE   And making bombs – but of course, not time bombs…

SAFIYA   Sound bombs.

VOICE   I've heard about them. The ones with terrible sounds that frighten people.

SAFIYA   No, no, no. Not one of those ordinary things. My handmade bombs were absolutely original.

VOICE   Can you explain it?

SAFIYA   Wouldn't be of any use to you. *(suddenly with great enthusiasm)* It's a kind of simple adjustment in the average intensity of a harmonic sound wave. The speed of sound at an average temperature is three hundred and thirty metres per second… its density is one-half kilogram per cubic metre. What I did was, I increased the pressure amplitude, and measured the low-frequency, large-amplitude displacement signals…

VOICE   Can you simplify your explanation a bit?

SAFIYA   *(loses her enthusiasm)* Simpler than this is impossible. Physics cannot be explained with the words that are used in a recipe for chickpea soup. *(silence)*

VOICE   I… I didn't mean any harm.

SAFIYA   In Algeria, no one means any harm…. She was always telling me to get married.

VOICE   Who?

SAFIYA   Mothers always love to see their daughters in a wedding dress. They don't mean any harm either.

VOICE   Why haven't you gotten married, Safiya? *(silence)* Do you hate men? *(silence)* Were your interrogators and torturers in Barbarous Prison men?

SAFIYA   Your voice…

VOICE   What?

SAFIYA   It's too loud.

VOICE   I'm sorry. I keep forgetting that your ears are very sensitive.

SAFIYA   It's not your fault. People, all people, love screaming so much.

VOICE   A psychological statistic indicates that forty…

SAFIYA   Throw statistics away. I've seen them, in demonstrations, in public speeches, in meetings. Their mouths wide open and their eyes bursting out of the sockets from the excitement.

VOICE   You don't like them?

SAFIYA   I think they're the ones who don't like me.

VOICE   Why? Why do you think that?

SAFIYA   Because I'm certain that they have never foamed in their lifetimes. Even once.

VOICE   Can you explain this more clearly?

SAFIYA   The people were screaming on the streets, "Down with the French!" I was covering my ears and running to that dark basement in the Deli Abraham neighbourhood, where it was quiet, so quiet.

VOICE   In the last three years, since the revolution ended, your ear problem should have been solved. People have been screaming less…

SAFIYA   *(all of a sudden, intimately)* How old were you when you got married?

VOICE   I was…

SAFIYA   Twenty-one? Twenty-two? Twenty?

VOICE   Twenty-seven.

SAFIYA   *(still intimately)* Isn't that a bit late for an Algerian girl?

VOICE   Well, I was studying…

SAFIYA   Medicine?

VOICE   A branch of medical science, pathology.

SAFIYA   I'm not thirty yet. Did you know that?

VOICE   Yes. It's in your file.

SAFIYA   *(Her sense of intimacy fades.)* Yes… file. I forgot about that. What about the number of electrodes? Is that in the file, too?

VOICE   What?

SAFIYA   *(quickly)* The number of electrodes that they hooked up to us.

VOICE   Safiya, calm down.

SAFIYA   *(frightened)* Was I too loud?

VOICE   In a way, you were…

SAFIYA   This is a matter of life and death. Tell me, please. Was I too loud, Doctor?

VOICE   Tell me. Were you tortured with electricity before the revolution? The machine that's called the Gegen?

SAFIYA   *(starts singing a revolutionary anthem)* "From our mountains…"

VOICE   Safiya, you're not feeling well…

SAFIYA   *(continues singing)* "The voices of free men are rising…"

VOICE   What's the matter, Safiya.

SAFIYA   "From our mountains…"

VOICE   Safiya… *Safiya!*

SAFIYA   *(covers her ears)* Don't scream for God's sake…. For God's sake.

VOICE   Oh… I'm sorry.

SAFIYA   *(shows her palm, which is red with blood)* Can you see it?

VOICE   Is it blood?

SAFIYA   Blood and dirt. Have you ever used Emo laundry detergent?

VOICE   Well, yes… I've washed my clothes with it a few times.

SAFIYA   I've eaten it a few times. The powder…

VOICE   You've eaten it?

SAFIYA   It's salty at first. Then becomes bitter… don't waste your time looking for it. There is nothing written about the taste of this powder in the file.

VOICE   Poor girl…

SAFIYA   Not so poor. I was the one who put the bomb in The Hearty Cook, as well as Le Faculté.

VOICE   Did your mother know that you had been tortured?

SAFIYA   I got used to seeing those five men: an inspector, an interrogator, the cord bearer and two in grey. But that day…. *(a brief sigh)* Do you know that I'm not thirty yet?

VOICE   I know.

SAFIYA   I wish I were. I wish I were thirty…. Forty…. Fifty…. Sixty!

VOICE   Why?

SAFIYA   So no mother would ask for a grandson from her daughter…

VOICE   You can't get pregnant?

SAFIYA   Have you read history?

VOICE   Why are you constantly jumping from one subject to another?

SAFIYA   It's said that for ten years after Ben Yousif conquered the cities, mothers couldn't guarantee their daughters were virgins at their weddings.

VOICE   Well, our history is full of carnage, rapes and massacre.

SAFIYA   You know the men of Deli Abraham and Kasbah…. Guys like Kamal and Morad didn't even give a damn about the electricity they passed through my body…. *(all of a sudden)* Yes, Mother!

VOICE   No one called you, Safiya.

SAFIYA   Yes, yes. That was her this time.

VOICE   But Safiya…

SAFIYA   There are sounds in the silence that you can't hear. If you would have spent a year in that smelly basement, like me—in absolute silence, working on the vibration amplitude of a fixed amount of frequencies, making your heart beat slower—then you would've known what I mean.

VOICE   Relax, Safiya…

SAFIYA   Do you remember the bombing of Le Faculté? I sent eighteen French men and women flying in ten seconds.

VOICE   I read it in the papers…

SAFIYA   Nonsense. No one knew what I did, no one – even the head of my unit. Everyone thought it was an ordinary sound bomb.

VOICE   Wasn't it?

SAFIYA   Of course not. My bombs didn't detonate with wires and clocks, they used vibration. My bombs didn't work in silence. But when its button was pushed with the first wavelength of opposing polarity… *(She whistles indicating an explosion.)*

VOICE   And what was this wavelength of opposing polarity?

SAFIYA   It was different in each explosion. The Hearty Cook bomb detonated with the screaming of the Kaiserslautern fans.

VOICE   And the Le Faculté bomb?

SAFIYA   That was more sensitive. I was told that a cute French girl always went to the gramophone to put on one of those Patachou songs. *(She sings quietly an old French song.)* Five! *(sings again)* Six! *(sings again)* Seven! *(sings)* Eight! *(sings)* Nine! *(sings)* Ten! *(Covers her ears.)* Did you hear it?

VOICE   So we can conclude that the victims themselves detonated your bombs.

SAFIYA   That's right. With their shouts and screams…

VOICE   But you can't take away the people's right to shout. With that shouting, the people won the revolution. Shouting out our belief means resistance, protest and struggle for freedom.

SAFIYA   Don't lecture me on resistance and struggle, lady. They peeled my skin off for four years in the French prisons.

VOICE   It's written three years in your file.

SAFIYA   Add one more year that I spent in that wretched basement.

VOICE   But you struggled for your cause. Weren't the people a part of that cause?

SAFIYA   For me, the people are divided in two groups: those who have foamed, and those who haven't. I belong to the first group.

VOICE   I… I don't understand!

SAFIYA   I have been tortured with objects that are the ordinary objects in your daily life…. Rope, chairs, cigarettes, bottles, laundry detergent…. Please, don't call me so much, Mother!

VOICE   No one called you.

SAFIYA   My mother had always bought Emo laundry detergent and talked constantly about its benefits… how clean it made the clothes, how economical it was… but no one ever told me about the taste.

VOICE   At first it's salty, and then it gets bitter.

SAFIYA   *(with a glimpse of hope in her face)* Have you tried it?

VOICE   No. You told me. And I'll tell everyone about it.

SAFIYA   Even your son?

VOICE   Even him. And I will tell him that the meaning of his name is a kind of local spice.

SAFIYA   *(like a child)* But don't tell him after eating the detergent powder, about what they did to me. Okay?

VOICE   Okay.

SAFIYA   *(as before)* Don't tell him that with a enema bag they filled my ears with water. Don't tell him that I saw foam coming out of my entire body. Out of my mouth, my ears, my skin, the bulbs of my hair. Even when I was crying it was foam instead of tears coming out of my eyes. No. Kids shouldn't know about these things.

VOICE   *(sadly)* Why?

SAFIYA   Because they're kids. But mothers have to know about so many things.

VOICE   What kind of things?

SAFIYA   Things that my mother didn't know.

VOICE   For example?

SAFIYA   *(proudly)* For example, I was an expensive prisoner for the French government.

VOICE   Really?

SAFIYA   I cost an extra twenty-five thousand francs for the police department.

VOICE   That much!?

SAFIYA *(counts)* Hours of overtime for the guards, interrogators and torturers, additional benefits for working on holidays, plus bonuses for the "special officer."

VOICE Special officer?

SAFIYA The sixth one who was added that day. May 27th, 1960. At 10:00 a.m.

VOICE How precisely you remember…

SAFIYA He told me, "You've already cost the government twenty-five thousand francs." His voice…

VOICE You still remember?

SAFIYA He took a bottle out of his pocket and said, "This is the last we're spending on you." …How much does a bottle cost?

VOICE Less than a franc.

SAFIYA Not too expensive. I thought it would be worth more then that. Do Kamal and Morad know this?

VOICE Your neighbours?

SAFIYA My suitors… wearing a white veil on the head means what?

VOICE Means happiness.

SAFIYA But I'm disgusted by whatever is white. My mother used to wash everything to make it white, the curtains, bedsheets, sofas. She covered everything with white sheets to protect them from dust. She constantly talked about the magical effect of Emo detergent powder. I was about to throw up.

VOICE That's why you went to Ahmad Blunsh's Electronics Shop on Rue Collinette on Friday, April 12th, 1962 at 5:00 p.m.?

SAFIYA How he had aged!

VOICE The same shop where you bought the equipment for your operations before the revolution…

SAFIYA The price of a puny wave finder was ten times more.

VOICE You bought the equipment and returned home…

SAFIYA I saw her sitting behind her sewing machine with lots of lace around her, all white.

VOICE What was she sewing?

SAFIYA I fixed the bobbin myself.

VOICE A white dress with a lot of lace…

SAFIYA   She called me, "Safiya, Kamal and his mother came here today again for the marriage proposal. What should I tell him?"

VOICE   And what did you say to her?

SAFIYA   "Tell Kamal the total number of electrodes cannot be counted."

VOICE   Safiya…

SAFIYA   Tell him that the bottle had the logo of Hôtel des Alps on it, where the rich people hold their wedding ceremonies.

VOICE   Calm down.

SAFIYA   Tell him my dowry is twenty-five thousand francs…

VOICE   Safiya…

SAFIYA   Tell him that Safiya is not expecting a white horse…

VOICE   Would you like a cigarette?

SAFIYA   Tell him that Safiya doesn't know, doesn't know, doesn't know why the price of a wave finder has to be so expensive and the price of a bottle so cheap.

VOICE   Safiya…

SAFIYA   Stop calling me, Mother. *(in tears)* Or at least don't yell my name.

VOICE   Don't cry…

SAFIYA   She had to yell my name. Did you know that?

VOICE   No.

SAFIYA   I lived in the furthest room in our house. I had sealed the windows with bricks so noises from outside wouldn't bother me. Mother had to scream my name so I could hear it.

VOICE   When did you start the operation? The same day or the day after Saturday?

SAFIYA   It's said that the laws of physics have been changing. Is this true?

VOICE   I don't know…

SAFIYA   But how can elastic waves, Newton's Second Law and the emission equation change?

VOICE   I don't know.

SAFIYA   But I know. Since a mother keeps calling her daughter, these laws stay the same.

VOICE   On Sunday, April 14th at 10:00 a.m.…

SAFIYA   The whole day, the sound of her sewing machine was in my head…

VOICE   She was sewing your bridal dress.

SAFIYA   The laws of fluid physics will remain intact for another thousand years.

VOICE   She was insisting that you get married as soon as possible.

SAFIYA   She knew more than twenty lullabies, when she was sitting behind the sewing machine...

VOICE   She didn't know of your torture stories in Barbarous Prison...

SAFIYA   It was décolletée, with so many pleats. She finished it on Saturday night. She called me to the mirror and held it in front of me. I wanted to tell her that I hate white... but...

VOICE   But what?

SAFIYA   I said, *(with fascination)* "How beautiful!"

VOICE   Was it?

SAFIYA   Fascinating. After six years, it was the first time I loved the white color. I was smiling and mother was crying with joy. She had succeeded. At that moment, I realized that I had to go through with it.

VOICE   Sunday morning, April 14th. What time did you start the operation?

SAFIYA   The sky of our neighbourhood is always grey. Even on sunny days. When I went to her room, she was still asleep. I looked at her. People look more beautiful when they're quiet. Did you know that?

VOICE   Did you kiss her?

SAFIYA   I was afraid to break her peace. Everywhere was like a beautiful dream.

VOICE   And then?

SAFIYA   For sure she had woken up, sitting behind the sewing machine. For sure she had murmured a lullaby. And then she had called me, "Safiya!" *(snaps her finger)* Click! It starts operating... five times fifteen to the power of negative three in joules per second per square metre becomes...

$$Ym = \frac{8 \times 10^{-4}}{7} = m$$

(calls) "Safiya." $Ym = 4 \times 10^{-8}\,m$

(calls) "Safiya!" A flock of crows pass over the house. *(calls)* "Safiya!" First the laces and diamonds and jewellery go up in the air. Then the sewing machine and the wedding dress... the bed sheets, all the white fabrics... the leg of a crow breaks forever...

Forever...

VOICE   Did you see her corpse?

SAFIYA   When I was a child I thought that crows didn't wash their clothes, that's why they were so black. Once I washed one of them with the Emo detergent powder. It died.

VOICE   Why did you kill her?

SAFIYA   Because she had thought I wasn't thirty yet. Isn't that ridiculous? ...Me!

VOICE   Then how old are you?

SAFIYA   Somewhere between one thousand and two thousand... around that...

VOICE   Aren't you tired? Don't you want to sleep?

SAFIYA   All those medications – don't you have a pill that can stop the bad dreams?

VOICE   Have you been having a nightmare?

SAFIYA   I'm seven and my hair is completely white. In my dream, I'm making the largest bomb in the world. The whole population of the world has circled around me but they're silent. They are scared. The cars are turned off. The drivers don't honk. The rally has stopped midway. Their fists are frozen in the air and their mouths left wide open...

VOICE   If this nightmare comes true one day... what then?

SAFIYA   And then... after six years... after six years...

VOICE   What would you do?

SAFIYA   I would scream.... (*She releases a scream from the bottom her heart, painful and heartrending.*) Stop calling me, Mother. (*the sound of a horrendous explosion*) Mother. (*another explosion*) Mother. (*explosion.*) Mother.

> *Lights fade out softly. But SAFIYA's voice calling "Mother" and the sounds of successive explosions go on, as if they continue to eternity.*

Playwright Bios

Playwright, filmmaker, theatre historian and university professor, **Bahram Beyza'ie** started skipping school from around the age of seventeen in order to go to movies, which were becoming popular in Iran at a rapid pace. This only fed his hunger to learn more about cinema and the visual arts. By 1961 he had already spent a lot of time studying and researching ancient Persian and pre-Islamic culture and literature. This led him to study Eastern Theatre and traditional Iranian theatre and arts, helping him to formulate a new non-Western identity for Iranian theatre. In 1969 he began his film career by directing the short film "Uncle Moustache" ["Amoo Sibilou"], followed by "Safar" in 1970. Immediately after, in 1971, he made his first feature film "Downpour" ["Ragbar"], which to this day is regarded by critics as one of the most successful Iranian films ever made. Since then he has produced and directed eight films, including "Stranger and the Frog" ["Gharibe va Meh"] (1974), "Ballad of Tara" ["Cherikeye Tara"] (1980), "Bashu, the Little Stranger" ["Basho Gharibeh Kochak"] (1986, released in 1989), "Another Time, Maybe" ["Shayad Vaghti Deegar"] (1988) and "Travellers" ["Mosaferan"] (1992). Although travelling abroad to France in order to do his work, Beyza'ie continues to live and work in his native Iran, facing considerable criticism and censorship from the Iranian government.

Abas Na'albandian's love of writing was shaped in his early years, helping his father sell newspapers on the streets of Tehran. He started writing at the age of eighteen. His first play *Research...* gained the attention of critics at the Art Festival of Shiraz, which at the time, was attracting internationally-recognized theatre creators such as Robert Wilson, Peter Brook and Jerzy Grotowski. But despite his early recognition, Na'albandian was never accepted by Iranian intellectuals, as he had little admiration for the movement of social realism in art that marked the end of the Shah's regime. Na'albandian's theatre was seen as too formalist and without purpose. Na'albandian's career, limited during the reign of the Shah, fared even worse following the Islamic Revolution. His work was banned, his plays destroyed, he was jailed several times, and was prohibited from leaving the country. He continued to translate and adapt Western pieces, including the work of Aeschylus and Peter Handke, but remained a broken man until his suicide at the age of forty-two.

Playwright, screenwriter and theatre director, **Mohammad Rahmanian**, was born in 1962. Rahmanian is considered one of the most important playwrights and theatre artists to emerge after the Islamic Revolution in Iran. He has written, adapted and directed numerous plays. Besides writing original work, he has also adapted and directed several plays by Western playwrights such as Jean Paul Sartre and Anton Chekhov. Rahmanian's plays and productions have travelled to many European cities and international theatre festivals including Sweden, Mexico, Ukraine, Romania, France, Azerbaijan and Turkey.

Rahmanian's plays are both deeply political and philosophical. The consistent themes in his work include social decay, violence and dehumanization in the face of war, revolution and occupation. His characters are the innocent and helpless victims of the narrow political and religious ideologies that have been imposed on them. The events of his plays usually take place in countries other than Iran – Algeria, England, Afghanistan. Due to his vast knowledge of both Western and Persian theatrical traditions, stylistically Rahmanian's work is a fusion of different theatrical styles.

Some of Rahmanian's critically acclaimed plays include *Fans* (2005), *The Resurrection of Love* (2006), *The Roster* (2001), *The Swan's Song* (2004), *The Heroes* (2004) and *A Play for You* (1998).

Contributor Bios

Soheil Parsa is an award-winning director, actor, writer, dramaturge, choreographer and teacher, whose professional theatre career spans twenty-nine years and two continents. In his native Iran, Soheil completed studies in theatre performance at the University of Tehran and began a promising career as an actor and director. Arriving in Canada with his family in 1984, Soheil completed a second Bachelor of Arts in theatre studies at York University and then went on to establish Modern Times Stage Company as one of the most exciting culturally-diverse theatre companies in Canada. As a director, set and stage designer, translator, adaptor, choreographer and actor, Soheil's work is based on his experience in Iran and focuses on oppression and loss of freedom (especially loss of speech). His art is created to empower those who are often marginalized and under-represented.

An actor and founding member of Modern Times Stage Company, **Peter Farbridge** has appeared in the majority of the productions of Modern Times including the title roles of Modern Times' productions of *Hamlet* and *Macbeth*. Peter participates in various aspects of the company's administrative and artistic process. Peter graduated from York University's theatre program in 1989 and began to work in the Toronto film, TV and theatre community. In 1992 Peter moved to Montreal

where he has been working in theatre and film both in English and French. Peter writes for theatre and for film, and has written and directed several documentary films as well as a short film scenario.

Brian Quirt is artistic director of Nightswimming and president of the Literary Managers and Dramaturgs of the Americas (LMDA). Brian directed the premiere of Anosh Irani's *Bombay Black*, named the outstanding new play of the 2005–2006 Toronto theatre season and nominated for the 2007 Governor General's Literary Award. Brian has been nominated for three Dora Awards, two for direction and one for his adaptation of the Iranian play *Aurash* with Soheil Parsa. He received the LMDA's 2003 Elliott Hayes Award for Dramaturgy in recognition of his work in creating and directing Nightswimming. His own works include the adaptations of Jane Urquhart's *The Whirlpool* and Michael Redhill's *Lake Nora Arms*, and the original play *The Death of General Wolfe*. He directed the premiere productions of two Jason Sherman plays, as well as Michael Healey's first play, *Kicked*, and is currently developing Judith Thompson's latest play through Nightswimming.